WAN

MYSTERY INVESTIGATORS

Are you looking for adventure? Are you curious? Do you like solving challenges — and, most of all, do you want to probe into some of the Great Mysteries of the World? Or, indeed, the universe?

YOU   RICHARD

Adventurous? ☐ Adventurous? (Adventure is fine as long as there are no big spiders . . . eek!)

Like a challenge? ☐ Like a challenge? (There's nothing I like better than really challenging challenges!)

Curious? ☐ Curious? (Oh yes! Some might say 'nosy'.)

If you can tick all the boxes, join me on a global journey to investigate the unexplained, the bizarre and the downright weird. From crazy crop circles and ancient desert drawings, to spaceship crashes and alien autopsies, you'll be stunned at some of the strange and spooky goings-on around the world . . .

All these mysteries have baffled the experts and left investigators clueless. My mission is to find out the truth. And I need your help.

Together, we'll weigh up the evidence, look at all the explanations — then you decide which is the best solution. You can even keep track of your solved mysteries by turning to page 109 and recording your verdict!

A word of warning: If you're the nervous type, put this book down now. Some of the mysteries we'll be investigating are pretty scary. The kind of things that might make a person a bit, well, jumpy . . .

What was that?

Did you hear something?

OK, I'd better calm down . . . and breathe . . .

Let's go. Time to explore the world's greatest mysteries!

Richard Hammond

RICHARD HAMMOND'S

GREAT MYSTERIES OF THE WORLD

ALIEN ENCOUNTERS

RED FOX

RICHARD HAMMOND'S GREAT MYSTERIES OF THE WORLD: ALIEN ENCOUNTERS
A RED FOX BOOK 978 1 849 41714 3

Published in Great Britain by Red Fox,
an imprint of Random House Children's Publishers UK
A Random House Group Company
1 3 5 7 9 10 8 6 4 2

Bind-up edition published by The Bodley Head 2013
This Red Fox edition published 2014

The Random House Group Limited supports the Forest Stewardship Council® (FSC®),
the leading international forest-certification organisation. Our books carrying the FSC label
are printed on FSC®-certified paper. FSC is the only forest-certification scheme supported
by the leading environmental organisations, including Greenpeace. Our paper procurement
policy can be found at www.randomhouse.co.uk/environment

MIX
Paper from
responsible sources
FSC® C016897

Set in Baskerville Classico 12/17.5pt

RANDOM HOUSE CHILDREN'S PUBLISHERS UK
61–63 Uxbridge Road, London W5 5SA

www.**randomhousechildrens**.co.uk
www.**totallyrandombooks**.co.uk
www.**randomhouse**.co.uk

Addresses for companies within The Random House Group Limited can be found at:
www.randomhouse.co.uk/offices.htm

THE RANDOM HOUSE GROUP Limited Reg. No. 954009

A CIP catalogue record for this book is available from the British Library.

Printed and bound in Great Britain by
CPI Group (UK) Ltd, Croydon, CR0 4YY

With special thanks to Amanda Li

CONTENTS

THE MISSION ...

... to find out the truth about Unidentified Flying Objects ...

BURNING QUESTIONS

🔥 Could UFOs be spaceships controlled by aliens?
🔥 Are they natural phenomena?
🔥 Why are they here?

MISSION DETAILS

What is a 'UFO' exactly? It's just what it says it is – a flying object that hasn't been identified. Now, there are a lot of 'objects' soaring around in the skies, and in space. Satellites, aeroplanes, birds, meteors, helicopters, weather balloons, even space junk (that's rubbish which has been left by humans to float around in space). As we know what these objects are, let's call them 'Identified Flying Objects' (IFOs).

But the really intriguing flying objects are the other kind – the UNIDENTIFIED ones. We have no idea what they are – or where they come from ...

UFOs can appear as glowing balls of light hovering in the air, metallic saucers whizzing through the clouds or triangular vessels blasting through the skies.

The classic UFO – can't think why they're often called 'flying saucers'!

Sightings have been reported by members of the public and by pilots for many years.

THE LOCATION

Anywhere! Just look up into the sky and you've got as good a chance as anyone else of spotting a UFO. They can appear at any time, in any part of the world. So keep looking up at the skies if you want to see one for yourself (but, obviously, try not to walk into a lamppost).

UFOs watch out!

UFOs can come in all shapes and sizes. Saucer-, sphere-, diamond-, cigar- and triangle-shaped objects have all been reported. Some UFOs have glowing lights. All of them fly. Different speeds have been reported, but many are said to move *really* fast – much faster than an aeroplane. Some UFOs hover around for a bit, then whizz away. Others perform impressive moves and turns, almost as if they're showing off to an audience.

THE EVIDENCE

Look back to ancient times and you'll find reports of strange unidentified objects in the skies from all over the world. A fourth-century Chinese manuscript talks of a 'moon boat' that appears every twelve years. In 217 BC ancient Romans saw what they described as shiny round 'shields' flying around in the sky. In 1211 a man called Gervase of Tilbury wrote of a floating ship appearing in the sky and later vanishing. And throughout history, mysterious flying objects have been depicted in great works of art.

© PHOTO SCALA, FLORENCE

It's behind you! This fifteenth-century Madonna has a close encounter with a spiky UFO – or is it a conker? (Madonna with Saint Giovannino – Domenico Ghirlandaio)

During the Second World War, bemused fighter pilots reported seeing glowing balls of light flying close to their planes. They even named them – *foo fighters*. (Years later, a rock group liked the name so much, they 'borrowed' it!)

The weird spheres whizzed and bobbed around and were like nothing the pilots had ever seen before. At first, Allied pilots thought they might be some kind of secret enemy weapons. But when the war was over, it was discovered that German pilots had also witnessed the 'foo fighters' – and they too thought they were enemy missiles! Both sides were wrong. No one ever worked out what the glowing balls were and they remain a mystery to this day . . .

Dancing Discs

Let's go back to 1947, when the world went UFO-crazy. It all started in June, when an American pilot called Kenneth Arnold had a very strange experience. While flying a plane over the Cascade Mountains in Washington, USA, a flash of light caught his eye at a height of about 3,000 metres. Arnold watched, fascinated, as nine shining, disc-shaped objects flew in formation through the clouds, not far from his plane. They were moving incredibly fast. He even timed them, later working out that the objects must have been travelling at a speed of 2,700 kilometres per hour – unbelievably fast and way beyond the ability of any plane that existed at the time!

Arnold was sure that the shiny objects were not made by humans. He said they moved like 'saucers skipping on water'. It

was from this description that the phrase 'flying saucers' began to be used, especially by the newspapers, who were reporting the story all over the world.

So why should we believe Kenneth Arnold? He was interviewed by US Military Intelligence and found to be a reliable witness and an intelligent, sensible man – not really the kind of person who goes around making up stories about seeing spooky spaceships. To this day, people have tried to find logical explanations for what Arnold saw – raindrops, pelicans, meteors and snowy mountain peaks have all been suggested – but to no avail. The Arnold case is still stored away in a file marked UNEXPLAINED.

Kenneth Arnold keeps a lookout in case more UFOs turn up...

The UFO Explosion

Just a few days after Kenneth Arnold's sighting, an airline crew spotted more discs in the skies over Idaho. And in early July, eight circular objects were seen whizzing around in the skies of Tulsa, Oklahoma. They weren't the only ones. All in all, hundreds of UFO sightings were reported across the USA. What was happening? Was the USA being invaded by hordes of alien spaceships – or had people's imaginations been sparked by Arnold's story?

Among all these sightings was the famous Roswell Incident of July 1947, when a spaceship was thought to have crashed into the desert (for more on this mystery, see page 23).

Since 1947, many hundreds of UFOs have been spotted by witnesses around the world. Here are just a couple of stories that stand out . . .

The glowing lights of Tulsa – just one of many UFO sightings in 1947.

The Lubbock Lights

This was the name given to some strange lights that were seen in the skies over Lubbock, Texas, in August and September 1951.

These shining lights were seen by many people, over three different nights. They flew in a V-shape and looked like bright, shining pearls. Some witnesses reported seeing eight or so lights, others as many as 30. All agreed that they moved incredibly fast, passing through the sky in a matter of seconds. A teenager called Carl Hart Jr managed to take some photographs of the weird lights (see the next page). The snaps showed eighteen to twenty mysterious objects flying in a neat formation.

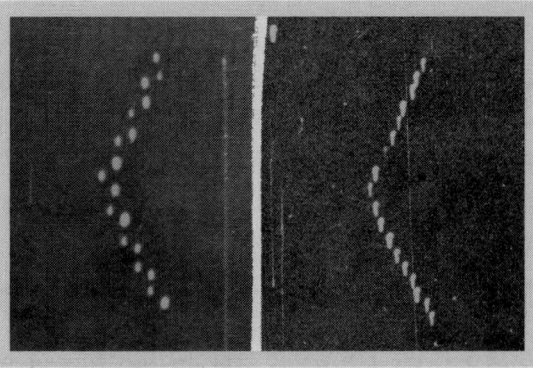

Carl Hart Jr's snap of the Lubbock lights – could they be birds – or something stranger...?

To this day, no one has an explanation for the Lubbock lights. At first it was thought they were lights from planes, but investigations at the nearby air-force base revealed that no planes were flying on the nights that the lights were spotted. Strange . . .

A later report said that they must have been birds with 'street lights reflecting from them'. This explanation came from the first ever official UFO report – Project Blue Book.

Project Blue Book

With files literally bursting with UFO sightings, it was time for the authorities to launch a proper investigation. Project Blue Book, as it was named, would look at every report of alien contact and UFO sighting in the USA. It wasn't a small job. More than 12,000 cases were investigated between 1948 and 1969 – 21 years. Well, no one can say that they didn't spend enough time on it . . .

Most sightings were said to be no more than clouds, birds, lightning, weather balloons or similar (boring) explanations. But that still left the cases the authorities *couldn't* explain – a whopping 700 of them. Those pesky UFOs just wouldn't go away . . .

Believe It or Not!

It wasn't just the USA that kept detailed files of UFO sightings. The United Kingdom did the same. And in 2011 these 'Top Secret' files from the Ministry of Defence were opened up to the public for the first time. They revealed 8,500 pages of UFO sightings, photographs and drawings sent in by the public. A staggering 11,000 UFO reports had been logged between 1959 and 2007. Some of the sightings were bizarre – one woman said she had seen a dome-shaped object landing and was then measured by two tall figures dressed in silver!

Others were less than convincing. One man told the authorities that he had seen a cigar-shaped UFO hovering above his house. He was sure that he must have been kidnapped by aliens. Why? Because he noticed that he had gained an extra hour of time and couldn't understand why. (These kinds of 'time-slips' are sometimes described by those who say they have been taken to a spaceship.) However, the report 'deduced' that the clocks had gone back that night! Duh!

Another report described a major 'alien alert' that happened in 1967. On the morning of 4 September the police and RAF were bombarded with calls from members of the public who had seen six saucers flying in a perfect line across southern England.

The authorities moved fast. Four police forces, a bomb-disposal unit, the army and intelligence officers were alerted, steeling themselves for a possible alien invasion. A military helicopter was despatched to intercept the possibly hostile flying extra-terrestrials.

It wasn't until the bomb-disposal squad found one of the 'UFO's on the ground and realized it was a fake that the whole thing was revealed to be a massive practical joke. Some engineering students from Farnborough Technical College had made the flying saucers as part of their college Rag Week. I expect the army, police and bomb-disposal squad were rolling about on the floor laughing at that one . . .

But even allowing for silly jokes, hoaxes and mistakes, just like America's Project Blue Book, the British files revealed many cases where no explanation at all could be found. And those cases are still open . . .

TRACKING THE TRIANGLE

Sometimes it's hard to be sure if a person's story is true or not. But when several witnesses see the same thing, it's a different matter.

On 29 November 1989 many people living in northern Belgium reported seeing a large triangular shape with lights underneath it

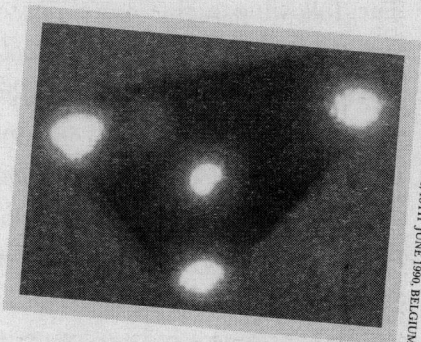

© J.S. HENRARDI, 15TH JUNE 1990, BELGIUM

moving across the sky. Its progress was tracked by locals and the police from the Belgian city of Liège across to the borders with Germany and the Netherlands.

Sightings continued up until April 1990, and the low-flying craft was seen hundreds of times. At one point, the mysterious shape appeared on radar screens at Belgian air-force bases. It was chased by fighter planes, but the weird craft kept changing direction and disappeared before it could be properly investigated. The pilots and air-force staff said that it had reached the most incredible speeds. No one has ever got to the bottom of the triangular phenomenon and it remains a complete mystery.

THE RENDLESHAM INCIDENT

On a dark night in December 1980 strange moving lights were seen above Rendlesham Forest in Suffolk, England. US Air Force personnel who were stationed nearby came to investigate the mysterious lights, thinking that a plane might have crashed nearby. They found burn marks on the trees and ground, and broken branches strewn around – but no plane.

The following night, more mysterious lights were seen by several witnesses. One of them, Colonel Halt, has since gone on to say he believes that the lights he saw were 'extra-terrestrial in origin' – in other words, made by aliens. He described one of the lights as looking like a large moving red eye. It apparently separated into several small white objects that flew off in different directions. Would you have hung around to get an eyeful of that?

Later, one of the servicemen who had also witnessed the incident, a Sergeant Jim Penniston, claimed to have seen – and touched – an actual spacecraft in the woods. He even made a sketch of what it looked like – a triangular craft with writing on the side that looked a bit like Egyptian hieroglyphics. However, none of the other witnesses could back up Penniston's sighting, and the spacecraft itself was never found.

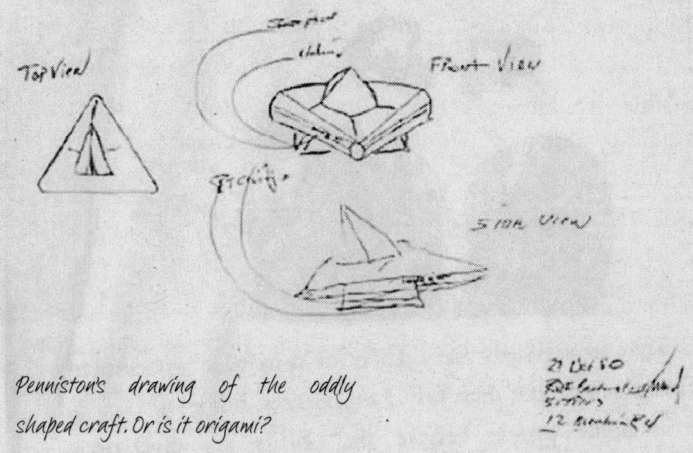

Penniston's drawing of the oddly shaped craft. Or is it origami?

Some UFO researchers believe that the Rendlesham sightings, which took place over two nights, are classic examples of 'close encounters' – real-life encounters with alien spacecraft.

Even stranger, all the files and documents about the Rendlesham incident have since disappeared from the Ministry of Defence Archives. Some believe that the case was covered up by the authorities and the files hidden from the public. In fact, some people believe that the truth about UFOs and aliens is being covered up by governments all around the world . . .

The Men in Black

The Men in Black mystery was around years before Will Smith landed his part in the blockbuster movie. Since the 1950s, stories have been told in the USA of anonymous figures dressed in smart black suits who turn up uninvited at the homes of people who have reported UFO sightings.

Unlike Will Smith, these MIBs don't do funky rapping.

Men in Black — smart but sinister ...

They are seriously scary. Their job is to 'warn' witnesses to stay quiet about their UFO experiences. But why?

Some people believe that MIBs are mysterious government agents who are being sent out to keep top-secret information, well, top secret ...

Others think that they are actually aliens sent to Earth to keep humans quiet about alien and UFO activity they have witnessed.

Wherever these sharp-suited figures come from, many UFO believers are convinced that the Men in Black really exist. So if you ever see a UFO and report it, don't be too surprised if you hear a knock at your door ... and if you do, don't look at their pen; you'll forget everything. Or maybe you already have ... ?

MY MISSION

Just how will I find a UFO? Well, it's going to be tricky. As I said earlier, you never know where or when an unidentified flying object might appear. The important thing is to be ready and waiting . . .

So I have decided to go on 'UFO Watch', using the loft of my house as a mini space observatory. I'm going to need some gadgets . . .

KIT LIST

 **LARGE WINDOW** – for maximum viewing of the skies

 **CAMERA WITH SUPER-ZOOM LENS ON A TRIPOD** – for capturing the evidence at first hand; a sturdy tripod mount will minimize image shake

 **CAMCORDER WITH DIGITAL ZOOM** – to record a moving UFO

 **TELESCOPE** – a top-of-the-range refracting astronomical telescope with slow-motion controls, to help keep any fast-moving UFOs in focus

 **COMFY SWIVEL CHAIR** – well, there's no point being uncomfortable, plus you can whizz around really fast to catch a glimpse of something interesting

 **PHONE** – to contact friends/witnesses

 LOGBOOK AND PEN – to make detailed notes of sightings

 **UFO ID CHART** – a reference for the various shapes of UFOs

 **SMALL JAR AND SPOON** – for taking soil samples at the site of a suspected UFO landing

I've got a few more ideas to help make my search as effective as possible:

TOP TIPS FOR UFO WATCHERS

1. If you can, ask some friends to join you on UFO Watch – or have them on autocall to get round to your place ASAP. Why? Because UFO reports are so much more believable when there are lots of witnesses to the event. It means you'll get taken seriously, and not laughed at. Which can happen. Trust me.

2. If you do see a UFO, naturally you'll be very excited. But try to stay calm and focused. Get evidence by taking a photograph or a film of the object. Try to include other things in the picture – buildings, planes, people; anything close by that will give an idea of the size, location and scale of your UFO.

3. It's important to make notes of as many details as possible. Directly after you've witnessed the UFO, write down the

exact time and how long you viewed it for. Describe the UFO – its shape, size, colour and estimated speed. Did the UFO have lights? Did it move around in an unusual way or change direction?

All this information is vital, so make notes while everything is still fresh in your mind. Why not draw a sketch of your UFO too?

MISSION COMPLETED

After several nights on 'UFO Watch' I've become something of an amateur astronomer and have spent hours viewing the crater-ridden surface of the Moon through my hi-tech telescope. Fascinating stuff. But did I see any UFOs? Well – I'm just not sure.

At 23:22 hours on the second night I caught sight of a glowing light moving through the night sky. It was fast – and very far away in the distance. The light was a yellowish colour and it left a slight trail behind it, which soon faded away.

I moved quickly, called my friends, but the light disappeared after two or three seconds – not enough time to get that vital shot or for my witnesses to do any witnessing. But I did make those all-important detailed notes in my logbook. (Pat on the back to me.)

So what could my mysterious object have been? It may well have been a shooting star – but there's always the chance that it could have been a genuine UFO. Another case for the MoD files . . .

WHAT DO YOU THINK?

So now it's up to you. What do you think is at the bottom of the UFO mystery? Here are your choices:

1. UFOs Are Sent by Aliens

As we've seen, many UFOs do have logical explanations, whether it is a bird, a plane or just a trick of the light. But there are always a small number of cases that just *cannot* be explained. In about five to ten per cent of UFO cases, the flying object remains a mystery. These are the ones that could be genuine UFOs – by that, I mean objects that have come from other planets or worlds.

We've also seen that UFOs are not that hard to fake – all you need is a camera, a home-made 'saucer', a blurry shot, and you've got yourself a pretty convincing photo. There's no doubt that the world of UFOs definitely has more than its fair share of hoaxes. But even so, how can cases such as the Belgian UFO sightings of 1989 be explained? It's difficult to see how hundreds of people – including the police – who all saw exactly the same thing, at the same time, could be fooled.

Let's look at the descriptions of UFOs themselves. They don't seem like anything made by humans. Most of them look unlike any kind of human craft and they move in a completely different way. Often they travel faster than any plane could manage. Is this proof that something non-human is behind them?

Some think that UFOs might be a kind of hi-tech device, remotely controlled by intelligent aliens. Perhaps they are using the devices to study humans and make notes about our strange species? If so, I wonder what conclusions they've come to?

The suggestion has even been made that UFOs are not spacecraft, but some kind of portal or 'wormhole' in our universe – a connection between different areas of space and time. Intelligent aliens – and they would have to be a whole lot cleverer than us – could maybe have worked out how to use wormholes to travel to different parts of the universe. A bit like the Tardis in *Doctor Who*. Which is definitely a VUFO – that's a 'Very Unusual Flying Object'!

But if UFOs *do* contain aliens, why haven't they let us know? Wouldn't it make sense not to be so secretive and to try and communicate with us properly? What are the aliens trying to hide?

Whatever you think, there's no doubt that many people truly believe that UFOs are connected to aliens. Some even spend their time researching UFO evidence. They call themselves Ufologists. They take it extremely seriously, even though Ufology is not accepted as a proper science.

But, as yet, even the Ufologists have not managed to come up with a real UFO, or a part of a UFO, or any other piece of evidence that would prove the link to aliens.

© POPPERFOTO/GETTY IMAGES

Is it a bird? Is it a plane . . . ? Doesn't look much like either to me. How do you explain this UFO spotted in New Jersey, USA?

2. UFOs Are All Explainable

There are many people who think that all UFO sightings can be explained by perfectly rational and logical reasons.

Apart from the usual birds and planes, there is another idea about what could be behind UFOs – and it doesn't involve aliens. It is a natural phenomenon called 'ball lightning'. Ball lightning definitely exists, but for years scientists have found it very difficult to explain.

It isn't like normal lightning. It appears as balls of electricity, fizzing with energy; apparently it looks like glowing tennis balls that dance and spin around in unexpected ways. The balls vibrate, produce sparks, and can even burn or melt nearby objects. They sometimes make a strange hissing noise and often appear during a thunderstorm.

Goodness gracious! Great balls of fire! This 1886 print proves that ball lightning is not a recent phenomenon.

© MARY EVANS PICTURE LIBRARY

How does it happen? One theory is that when lightning strikes certain surfaces, a vapour is formed. This vapour then condenses and mixes with oxygen in the air to slowly burn – which produces the weird ball effect.

It's easy to see how ball lightning could be the explanation for the 'foo fighters' of the Second World War and the many other strange glowing lights seen by people over the years. But how does it explain the different shapes of craft spotted by UFO witnesses – the ones that don't look like balls of light? Many of these have been seen flying in formation – could ball lightning really form itself into a neat triangle or V-shape?

Other explanations put forward for UFOs include meteors, also known as 'shooting stars'. When tiny rocks burn up in Earth's atmosphere, they create a fast-moving streak of light, which can be seen trailing across the night sky. Meteors are more common than you might think – apparently, on most nights, several meteors cross our skies. Ever spotted one?

Clouds have also been mistaken for flying saucers, particularly an unusual type called a 'lenticular cloud'. (Guess what – it's shaped like a lentil, which is a convenient way of remembering a fancy word!) Take a look at this:

Have you ever seen a cloud like this? It's easy to see why people think it's a flying saucer...

There's also the possibility that people are seeing things that aren't there – maybe a trick of the light or a hallucination? It's no coincidence that sightings of UFOs suddenly increased after Kenneth Arnold's famous incident. Were people imagining things because they had read about his story? The human mind can behave in some very strange ways . . .

YOU DECIDE

UFOs definitely exist – but are they being sent by creatures from other worlds? Make up your mind and jot down your thoughts at the back of the book. Don't forget to keep scanning those skies for your own evidence.

THE MISSION ...

... to find out if aliens have ever crash-landed on the Earth ...

BURNING QUESTIONS

🔥 Were aliens found in the US desert?

🔥 Was the whole thing a cover-up?

🔥 Just who is telling the truth?

MISSION DETAILS

In the summer of 1947 there was an accident in the desert in the state of New Mexico, USA. Nothing too unusual about that, you might think. But this incident was no ordinary one. It involved a speeding vehicle – but it wasn't a car. Many people believe that it was a spaceship. Steered by aliens. Which crashed into our planet. Here's a thought – perhaps they just couldn't find a parking meteor?!

There were witnesses to the crash, but no evidence. Some believe that this was because the military were told to quickly remove all signs of the accident.

23

Could a speeding spaceship really have hit our planet? Time to investigate . . .

THE LOCATION

This mystery is known, rather unimaginatively, as the Roswell Incident. Why? Because – yawn – it happened quite close to a city called Roswell. You know, just occasionally, I wish they'd think of more exciting names for these kinds of things – maybe the 'Exploding Spaceship Incident' or the 'Disappearing Aliens in the Desert Dilemma'? But for now, we're stuck with 'Roswell'.

Apart from the alien connection, Roswell is a fairly ordinary city located in the south-east of the state of New Mexico. The accident was said to have happened about 120 kilometres outside the city, in a quiet desert area.

Roswell also happens to be home to the New Mexico Military Institute – and the military play a large part in this story.

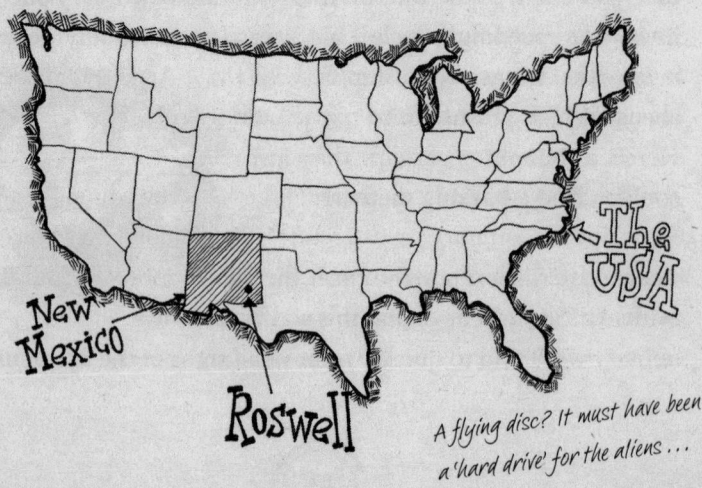

A flying disc? It must have been a 'hard drive' for the aliens . . .

THE EVIDENCE

Step forward our main witness – a rancher by the name of Mac Brazel. In June 1947 Mac rode out on his horse to check on his sheep (as you do if you're a sheep-owning rancher). As he trotted along, he noticed some strange-looking pieces of debris scattered around on the ground. He didn't think too much about them at the time, but later on, he wondered what the unusual bits and pieces might be. A couple of weeks later, he went back, picked some up and took them home.

It was weird stuff. Really strange. Apparently, there were pieces of what looked like thick tin foil – but it couldn't be torn, unlike normal tin foil. There were also what appeared to be pieces of wood with some weird, unknown writing on it. Mac and his family had never seen anything like it before.

There the story might have ended, had it not been for the fact that Kenneth Arnold's sighting of nine flying saucers was widely reported in the papers that week (see page 44). Like everyone else at the time, Mac heard the sensational news and wondered if the stuff he had found was somehow connected to the appearance of those shiny UFOs that Arnold had seen. He decided to show his find to the local sheriff.

The sheriff was mystified too, and together they contacted the authorities. A military investigator called Major Jesse Marcel came to Roswell to take a look at the scene. Soon after, all the debris was cleared away, leaving no trace of the incident.

Making the Headlines

The story didn't stay quiet for long. It was soon reported in the local paper that on 8 July US Military Intelligence had retrieved a 'flying disc' from the desert. This was incredible, world-changing news – a real flying saucer had actually been found! BUT the very next day the military changed their story. They said that it was all a big mistake and what had actually been found was a weather balloon. What a let-down!

How could the military have got this so wrong – surely a weather balloon couldn't be confused with a flying saucer? The sudden change in their story made people suspicious, and to this day, there are those who believe that the real truth was kept from the public.

Note: A weather balloon, by the way, is not your standard party balloon. It is a special kind of large balloon that is sent up into the atmosphere to retrieve information on temperature, wind speed, etc., to help make weather forecasts. It does not have HAPPY BIRTHDAY written on it.

More Witnesses Emerge

Strangely, in the same month, a Mr and Mrs Wilmot had been sitting outside on their porch in New Mexico, enjoying the peaceful evening. It was dark and quiet, but suddenly, out of the sky whizzed a glowing object. The Wilmots said it looked like two saucers glued together. Whatever it was, it had light glowing from inside and was moving incredibly fast (sound familiar?).

The Wilmots were pretty freaked out, and at first decided to keep the story to themselves – after all, they didn't want people thinking they were crazy. But they eventually broke their silence and told people what they had witnessed.

After the initial excitement, the story fizzled out. More than 30 years elapsed. That is, until 1978, when Major Jesse Marcel was interviewed – remember him? He was the intelligence officer who was sent to pick up the debris from the desert after Mac Brazel reported his find. Major Marcel admitted some very interesting things:

- The things that the military had found were like 'nothing made on this Earth'
- He described the 'foil' Mac had found as being like wafer-thin metal but incredibly tough. It was as light as balsa wood, but couldn't be cut or burned. Was it really a unique type of material made by aliens?

Following Marcel's revelations, 'Roswell Mania' erupted – magazine articles, TV programmes and books appeared, full of stories about aliens having visited Earth. More witnesses came forward and were interviewed. For example:

Lieutenant Walter Haut

Haut had been working at the military base in 1947 and he knew a lot about the case. After all, he was the person who issued the press releases following the crash. Haut died in 2005, but he left behind a signed written document –

with strict instructions that it was to be opened only after his death. What secrets did it contain?

As it happens, quite a lot. Among other exciting nuggets of information, Haut said:

- The weather-balloon story was a cover-up
- What had actually been found was an alien spacecraft. Haut had seen it with his own eyes, stored in an aircraft hangar called Building 84
- The craft was made of metal and shaped like an egg, around 4.5 metres long. There were no windows or doors on it
- On the floor were two bodies, partially covered. The bodies had very large heads and were only about 1.2 metres tall

Haut stated that he was convinced that what he'd seen was a craft from outer space and its (not very alive) alien occupants . . .

This was incredible . . .

Glenn Dennis

And there's more: in 1989 a man called Glenn Dennis (who used to be a mortician, so he knew a bit about dead bodies) came forward to say that he had been contacted by the authorities at Roswell shortly after the crash and asked to provide a number of 'child-sized' coffins. Weird . . .

Glenn made his way to the base, where he was apparently told by a nurse that she had seen the bodies of three small alien creatures. The nurse disappeared in mysterious circumstances soon afterwards, though some people have questioned whether she ever existed at all.

Area 51

Roswell isn't the only place where people suspect the authorities of hiding alien evidence. Area 51 is the name of a top-secret military base in the remote desert of Nevada, USA. It's so secret, we're probably not supposed to know it exists. And you can't visit – it's off-limits for everyone except certain military personnel and government officials.

Area 51 – the sign makes it pretty clear that you're not welcome . . .

We don't know what happens here, but UFO and alien believers have long suspected Area 51 of being a place where alien-related activities take place, away from the public gaze. Some theories about this are:

- It's where they hide crashed alien spacecraft
- It's a place where new technologies – such as time travel – are being developed, based on alien technology and information
- Meetings with aliens are held here

Stories about the mysterious Area 51 persist – wouldn't you just love to be a fly on the wall in that place?

THE SPY BALLOON STORY

Back to Roswell. It was time for a full investigation. Which is exactly what happened. In 1995 an official report finally came out. It confirmed that the crashed object definitely had been a weather balloon. So why all the secrecy? Well, this was no normal weather balloon. The report said that it was part of a top-secret government project called Project Mogul. Hi-tech, high altitude – and designed to detect sound waves from Russian nuclear bomb tests. In other words, it was a secret spy balloon! A sort of James Bond of the balloon world . . . having a real-life skyfall.

I've really let myself down

This would explain why all the debris was cleared away so quickly and why everything was kept so secret – the Americans didn't want the Russians to find out that they had been spying on them. Was this the real story behind Roswell? But despite this new information, the alien connection just wouldn't go away.

The So-called Alien Autopsy

In case you didn't know, an autopsy is an official examination of a dead body to find out why a person (or an alien) died. In 1995 an astonishing piece of film emerged, said to have been taken by a military officer in 1947, just after the Roswell crash.

It showed the body of what looked like a dead alien laid out on a table. With an over-sized head, large eyes and a small body – and twelve toes on each foot – it certainly looked like something out of this world. A person who looked like a surgeon, dressed in protective clothing, was performing an autopsy on the alien's body.

The film caused a sensation around the world. Here at last was *real evidence* – not only that aliens existed but that the authorities had kept the Roswell aliens secret for years. But questions remained. Why had the film been released only now? And how had Ray Santilli, the man who revealed the film to the public, got hold of it in the first place?

Here's a still from this remarkable movie. What do you think?

You can breathe out now – after much excitement and controversy, Ray Santilli later admitted that the film wasn't real He said it was supposed to be a

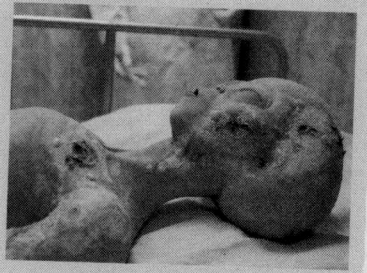

© PHOTO BEARD/SHUTTERSTOCK

The Roswell alien – not looking in the best of health.

'reconstruction' of what could have happened in Roswell. Looking at it again, there were a couple of obvious signs. Such as:

- 🌐 The alien looked like it was made of rubber
- 🌐 The so-called 'surgeons' weren't holding their instruments properly, as real doctors would

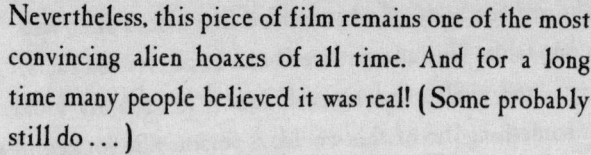

Nevertheless, this piece of film remains one of the most convincing alien hoaxes of all time. And for a long time many people believed it was real! (Some probably still do ...)

All of which proves that, these days, it's really not that hard to fake a piece of film. You just need a camera, some friends and an alien costume from a fancy-dress shop ...

MY MISSION

A visit to the city of Roswell would be a good start. Roswell also boasts its own UFO Museum and Research Center, so whatever happens, I can find out more about the case.

Looks like the ideal place to find out about UFOs ...

KIT LIST

 FACTOR-50 SUN CREAM AND SUN HAT – Roswell is in the desert, so it will be hot, hot, hot

 PLENTY OF WATER – don't want to dehydrate

 WIDE-ANGLE BINOCULARS – for checking out the skies and the desert landscape

 TWEEZERS – for picking up any bits of interesting debris

 MAGNIFYING GLASS – for close-up examination

 COLLECTION BOX – always best to keep any evidence for future use

 ROSWELL INFORMATION BOOKS – there are lots of them, so I'll take a few to read on the plane

MISSION COMPLETED

I arrived at Roswell – hot, humid and jet-lagged – to find the entire city overrun by aliens! Had the original crash-landed aliens survived, settled down and had kids?

A closer inspection of the aliens revealed the truth. They were humans – dressed up in some pretty incredible outfits. It seems that, since the events of 1947, the city of Roswell has become the 'alien capital' of the world.

Even the local burger joint looks like a flying saucer!

And every year, in July, the town celebrates 'Alien Month' with a one-week festival. People dress up as aliens, there are parades, concerts, even puppet shows. Here are a few of the locals joining in with the festivities.

As my visit coincided with this festival, I felt in need of an alien costume to blend in with the locals. There was nothing left to hire so I made do with a pair of deely boppers, some green face

Greetings, Earth boy! Take me to your leader . . .

paint and a last-minute sheet borrowed from my hotel room. Don't ask why I had the deely boppers and green face paint in my bag, I just did, OK?

Once the festivities were over, I hired a four-by-four, and drove out to the spot where the crash was supposed to have happened. As the site had been so thoroughly cleared all those years ago, I wasn't really expecting to find any debris or shiny foil. And guess what – I didn't. The desert stretched out for miles around Roswell, and there was no sign of any alien activity – just a lot of bushes. But bearing in mind that this all happened in 1947, it's probably not that surprising.

The desert landscape – not a UFO, or even an IFO, in sight.

WHAT DO YOU THINK?

Let's look at the facts of the case:

1. Something crashed into the desert that day.
2. The military changed their account of what happened.

So you need to make a decision. Here are your choices:

1. The Object Was an Alien Spaceship

There are several witnesses who are convinced that they saw real aliens, and even a real spaceship. But some think that Haut and other witnesses made everything up – perhaps to get attention or to make money from selling their story. But why would someone like Lieutenant Walter Haut, a respectable military man, make it up? And why would he have left his signed document to be read *after* his death? He would have gained nothing from it.

35

We also need to ask why Haut didn't reveal his sighting of the spacecraft and the aliens earlier in his life. But there's a simple explanation for that – he probably thought that people would laugh at him or think he was crazy. That's why he wanted the truth to come out after he was gone.

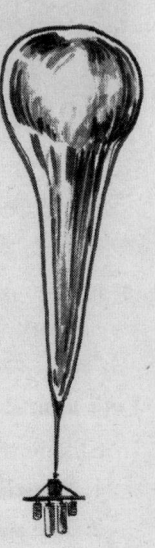

There's also the question of the debris that Mac Brazel found – did it come from a spy balloon or a spaceship? If only we had a piece of that 'tin foil', it could be tested to find out its origin. But we haven't, so we can't.

There's no doubt that the authorities have changed their story several times, which makes people very suspicious. And the military were clearly anxious to get rid of any traces of the accident. But were they trying to cover up the fact that aliens had been found or to keep their spying activities secret? Which is more likely?

Ask yourself:
- Do you believe the stories of the witnesses?
- Do you think that the strange debris came from an alien ship?
- Do you think that the authorities were trying to cover up an alien crash?

If you've answered 'yes' to all the above, then you are a Roswell alien believer!

2. The Object Was a Spy Balloon

The fact remains that no one has been able to come up with actual evidence, such as a chunk of alien spaceship or an authentic photo of one of the alien bodies, to prove that the crashed object was a spaceship. Surely there would still be a piece of the debris that was found in 1947 left to analyse? Or a photo of one of the aliens that isn't a hoax? But there is nothing.

But what about the bodies of aliens that people said they saw? A second US Air Force report in 1997 stated that the witnesses were mistaken. It said what they actually saw was probably human-shaped test dummies that were carried by the balloon for scientific research. Do you believe that people would mistake dummies for aliens?

Is it likely that the object that crashed was a spy balloon, as the government said? It's certainly true that in 1947, both the USA and Russia were keeping their scientists busy by developing atomic bomb technology. Both countries would have desperately wanted to know what their rivals were up to. It's plausible that the spy balloon was a top-secret project that went wrong – which is why the government sent the military in fast to clear up the mess.

Has the Roswell incident been blown up into much more than it should have been? Your call . . .

YOU DECIDE

If you think the alien story is true, then the Roswell crash is one of the most important scientific discoveries ever made. But if you believe the authorities, it's all a big mistake.

Whatever you think, more than 65 years on, it seems that the name 'Roswell' will always be associated with aliens, conspiracy and secrets. Head to the back of the book to note down your theory . . .

THE MISSION . . .

. . . to find out who – or what – drew hundreds of giant pictures on the ground.

BURNING QUESTIONS

🔥 What do the drawings mean?
🔥 Did aliens make them?
🔥 Were they used as runways for alien astronauts?

MISSION DETAILS

I'm going in search of the Nazca Lines – a collection of mysterious lines and drawings which have had archaeologists baffled since they were discovered in the 1920s.

Why Are They So Puzzling?

1. They are really, really old. Experts think they were probably made between 400 and 650 AD.
2. Many of the lines and drawings are absolutely huge – some would fill a football stadium – even two! They can only be seen properly from a very high spot, preferably from a plane.

(And, in case you didn't know, planes hadn't been invented between 400 and 650 AD!)

3. No one is really sure who made them – and for what reason.

Actually, the name 'Nazca Lines' is slightly misleading because these amazing works of art are not just lines. There are also geometric shapes, trees, flowers, humans, a monkey, a spider, a hummingbird, fish, a jaguar, a lizard, a dog – even a killer whale! The largest drawing is a 285-metre pelican (I bet you've never seen one of those before!). All are really impressive and beautifully made.

© TRAVELPIX/ALAMY

A 93-metre-long hummingbird soars across the desert floor.

How did the ancient people – or beings – who made them do such precise drawings on such a massive scale?

Let's go on the Nazca trail . . .

THE LOCATION

Sandwiched between the coast and the Andes mountain range of Peru lies the Nazca Desert. If you ever visit, take plenty of water, as this is one of the driest places in the world. In fact, the very dry atmosphere is one of the reasons why the Nazca Lines have survived intact for so many hundreds of years.

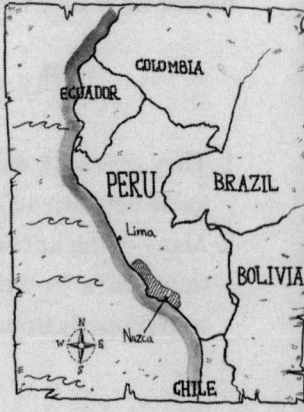

The part of the desert where the Nazca Lines are found is called the Pampa Colorada, an 80-kilometre-long plateau running parallel to the Pacific Ocean. Its name means the 'Red Plain', so called because the area is covered in reddish-brown stones.

THE EVIDENCE

The Nazca Lines are what's officially known as geoglyphs. If you've ever made a picture out of pebbles on the beach, you will have created your very own geoglyph – it's a piece of art made by arranging stones or earth on the ground.

The Nazca geoglyphs were spotted in the late 1920s, around the time that air travel started to become more common.

The lines are an amazing sight, and people come from all over the world to view the ancient wonder. There are hundreds of lines, triangles, quadrangles, zigzags and circles, as well as creatures of land, air and sea.

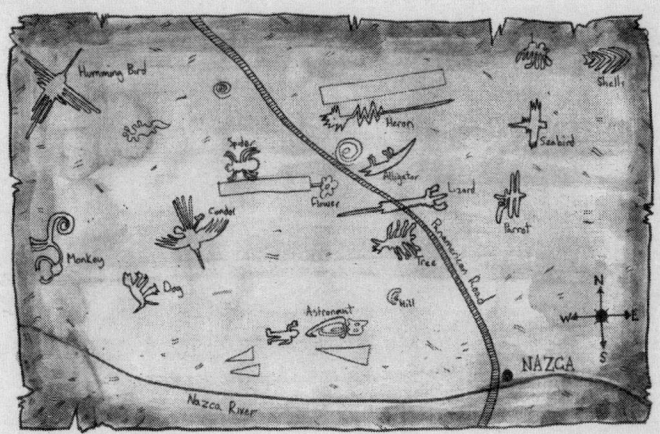

A map showing part of the virtual 'zoo' in the Nazca Desert.

How Were the Lines Made?

No paint or chalk was used to make the drawings – they have literally been scratched onto the ground. A closer inspection reveals that the reddish-brown stones on the desert surface have been skilfully cleared away to reveal the lighter soil underneath. Each line is up to 30 centimetres deep. It's as if the desert has been used as a giant drawing pad!

Now, if you've ever tried to paint a really big picture, you'll know just how difficult it is to get the size and scale right. How did these drawings get made so precisely when they were done so long ago – a time when people didn't have planes or computers or other modern technology to help? This is something that has been puzzling experts for a long time.

And as the best way to see the shapes is to fly above them, this has led to the suggestion that aliens might have been involved with their creation . . .

Beware of the world's biggest spider!

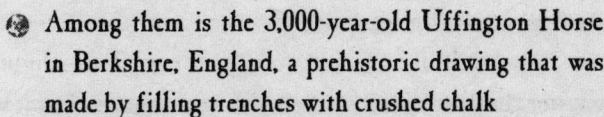

Great Geoglyphs

The Nazca Lines are the most famous geoglyphs in the world, but there are many others.

- Among them is the 3,000-year-old Uffington Horse in Berkshire, England, a prehistoric drawing that was made by filling trenches with crushed chalk
- The mysterious Marree Man in South Australia was only discovered in 1998. It is massive – 4.2 kilometres high – and no one has any idea who made it or when
- The Atacama Giant is found in the Atacama Desert of Chile, where there are many other geometric and animal pictures – even a giant llama! The giant is 119 metres tall and is believed to have been made between 600 and 1500 AD
- There are also huge geoglyphs in Egypt, Malta, the United States (Mississippi and California) and Bolivia. Perhaps there are more waiting to be discovered . . . check the back garden

Looking into the Lines

Since the discovery of the Nazca Lines, teams of experts have travelled to the desert to investigate. There have been many ideas about what the lines could have been used for, from ancient racetracks to landing strips for aliens – more on all these later!

As you can see from the spider on page 42, most of the drawings are made from one single continuous line. The lines never cross each other, which some think may indicate that they were once used as pathways – perhaps for some kind of procession or ceremony?

Whatever they are, pretty much everyone agrees that it would have taken a very long time, and a lot of people, to plan and make them – possibly many, many years.

MY MISSION

My trip to Peru kicks off with a flight to its capital city, Lima. From there I can drive the 400 kilometres or so south to the Nazca Desert. It'll be very hot and dry, so my desert survival kit will be vital.

I won't be able to walk around the lines because they are now a protected area and a UNESCO World Heritage Site. It's fair enough – even though they have survived in the desert for 2,000 years, hundreds of tourists trampling over them would soon turn the Nazca Lines into 'non-existent' lines.

To see the lines you can climb a special viewing platform or fly over them in a small single-engine light aircraft. The view might be better from the plane, but I hear that the flight can be very turbulent in the hot, strong desert winds. Turbulence is bad – and I really don't fancy spending the flight with my head in a sick-bag. So – the viewing platform it is . . .

KIT LIST

 MAP – I really don't want to get lost in the desert

 COMPASS – in case I get lost in the desert . . .

 WATER – as much 'agua' as I can possibly carry

 CAMERA WITH WIDE-ANGLE LENS – for taking the best shots of the lines in the desert landscape

 BINOCULARS – for viewing the lines from a distance

 SUN HAT AND SUNGLASSES – a 'must' in the desert

 SUN-SCREEN – the highest factor I can get

 SIGNALLING MIRROR – in case of emergency, I could use the mirror to signal for help: all you need are some sun rays (and there are plenty of those in the Peruvian desert) to bounce off the mirror's surface and you've got yourself a flashing light

 SPARE TYRE – having a tyre blowing out in the desert wouldn't be fun

 PETROL CAN – running out of petrol wouldn't be much of a laugh, either!

MISSION COMPLETED

After a long drive I eventually found the metal tower called the Mirador, which is by the side of the highway.

I climbed the steps to the top and had a good look around with my binoculars. From here I could see three of the famous drawings:

- A gigantic lizard
- A figure they call 'the Hands' (see below)
- A tree

The Mirador – that's Spanish for 'lookout' – is where you go to, er, look out!

They were huge – an amazing sight. The figure, in particular, was really strange. It looked like a weird unknown creature, maybe a bird. The hands were human-like, but one had only four fingers. Could this be some kind of alien creature?

My trip to the Nazca Lines has made me realize just what an amazing feat it was to create them. And it's left me wondering how on earth humans could have done it . . .

WHAT DO YOU THINK?

1. The Nazca Lines Were Made by Humans

Many archaeologists think that this is the case. The artists would have been the ancient Nazca people, who lived in the region from roughly 200 BC to about 600 AD. The driest desert in the world can't have been an easy place to live, but the nifty Nazcas seemed to have managed. They constructed irrigation channels to make the most of their limited water supplies and grew a variety of crops, such as corn, beans and cotton. Nice job, Nazcas!

Nazca Nasties

We don't know a lot about the Nazcas, but over the years, archaeologists have dug up some interesting objects that reveal a number of strange facts about their lives. Things like decorated bowls, patterned textiles, musical instruments – and the largest collection of severed heads in Peru ...

Most of these skulls have holes drilled through the front of them. Rope was strung through the holes – experts think these were carrying ropes so that the heads could be 'worn', perhaps around the body. Very decorative ...

At first, the experts thought the heads must have come from those (unlucky) enemies killed during tribal battles, later worn by the Nazcas as 'war trophies'.

This kind of thing was known to have happened in other ancient civilizations. But on closer inspection, they were found to be heads of the Nazca people themselves! Why would they want to wear the heads of people they knew – maybe even those of friends and family? Was it some kind of bizarre fashion accessory or had everyone literally 'lost their heads'?

One theory is that the Nazcas liked to have 'offering heads' as sacrifices to the gods. The heads appear to come from both men and women, but no one knows why a particular person would have been chosen for the special honour of donating their head to a good cause ...

© STRINGER/ PERU/ X01495/ REUTERS/ CORBIS

Drilling holes into the skulls can't have been a 'hole' lot of fun!

Buried Nazca bodies have been found too, with their heads missing. And here's another thing you'll find it hard to get your head around: their heads had been replaced with a 'head jar' – a ceramic pot with a human face painted on it. Even more bizarre – there were small plants growing from the top of the jars! Jar hair, I suppose?

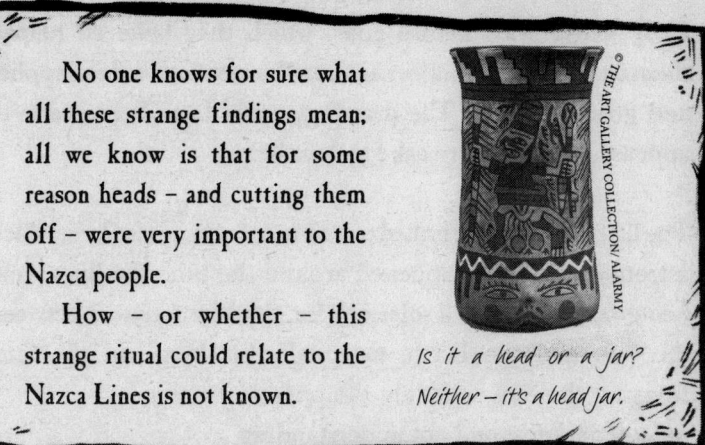

No one knows for sure what all these strange findings mean; all we know is that for some reason heads – and cutting them off – were very important to the Nazca people.

How – or whether – this strange ritual could relate to the Nazca Lines is not known.

Is it a head or a jar?
Neither – it's a head jar.

© THE ART GALLERY COLLECTION/ ALAMY

Whatever went on in the Nazca people's heads, creating the Nazca Lines would have been incredibly hard, complicated work – so if they were made by the Nazcas, they must have had a very good reason for making them. Archaeologists have come up with a few possible ideas:

Starstruck

One of the first people to properly research the Nazca Lines was a woman called Maria Reiche. She spent years studying them and became convinced that the lines were created as a huge star chart – a massive map of the sky and its constellations. She thinks this could have helped the Nazcas find important stars and predict planetary events, such as eclipses.

For the eyes of the gods

Think about it. Why is it that the lines are best seen from the sky? Perhaps they weren't made for humans to see at all? The Nazcas may have made them for their gods to look at.

They worshipped nature gods, which they believed helped them in important matters such as the weather, water supplies and growing crops. The drawings could have been made to appease the gods or to ask for their help.

The lines may also be linked to a series of eclipses in Peru, which astronomers think happened around the time the lines were being made. During a solar eclipse, the Moon passes between the Sun and the Earth, eventually blocking out the Sun. Imagine the Sun suddenly disappearing, being in total darkness and not understanding why? It must have been terrifying. Some think that the Nazca people believed that a giant eye was watching them from the sky. They may have thought that this eye caused the eclipses – a kind of giant 'blink' from God. Did they make the lines to please the 'eye in the sky'?

"Do you ever feel like you're being watched?"

Water works

What's really important if you live in one of the driest deserts in the world? Water, of course. One suggestion is that the lines pointed to places where water flowed under the desert floor, acting as a kind of 'water map' to help locate the precious liquid. Agriculture was crucial to the Nazca way of life – without water, their crops would have died and so would they.

Ancient racetracks

Another idea is that the lines were built as racetracks – like a kind of stadium for running races. The lines do look a bit like a series of winding paths. But no one is sure how they would have been used – and whether they were intended for animals or humans.

Probably the most convincing argument for the Nazcas being responsible for the lines is that some of the figures drawn in the desert are very similar to images found on Nazca pottery and art. Take a look at this jar, for example.

Birds and fish were often found on Nazca pottery – can you see any similarities between these and the Nazca Lines?

© DEA / G. DAGLI ORTI

2. The Lines Were Made by Aliens

In 1968 Swiss author Erich von Däniken wrote what was to become a very famous book. It was called *Chariots of the Gods?* In the book he put forward the idea that the lines were landing strips for alien spacecraft. He thought that they were too complex to have been drawn while standing on the ground – so he argued that they must have been made from the air. But as ancient cultures did not have aeroplanes, he believed that only aliens flying in spacecraft could have mapped out the lines. Some have suggested that the Nazca people could possibly have used hot-air balloons to get up into the sky and map out the pictures – but no evidence has been found that they ever went ballooning.

Many of von Däniken's readers agreed with his idea that alien astronauts visited humans in ancient times. They think that the aliens were welcomed – even worshipped as gods – and that they could have given humans in many parts of the world the knowledge to create wonderful buildings and structures.

How else would so many ancient cultures have achieved such incredible feats – things that should have been impossible? Feats like the building of the Great Pyramids in ancient Egypt, constructing the circle of Stonehenge in Great Britain and, of course, making the Nazca Lines (among many others). The alien believers argue that they must have had help from more advanced, intelligent beings. However, many historians think that there were other, clever, ways in which humans managed to achieve these feats.

Strangely, one of the Nazca drawings shows a mysterious figure that has been named 'the Astronaut'. Take a look. What do you think? Could this be one of the visiting alien 'astronauts' who helped make the lines in the first place?

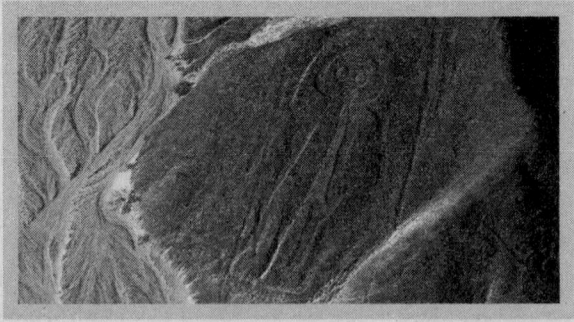

The Astronaut is 3.2 metres tall and looks like he might be feeling a bit queasy ...

Alien ancestors

If you ever visit the Nazca Desert you'll see that there are hundreds of crisscrossing, zigzag and parallel lines going in many directions and extending way out into the desert. They do look a bit like runways or landing strips, though they wouldn't make any sense to a human pilot. But to a creature from another planet – maybe?

© PHILIP SCALLIN/ALAMY

Is it a bird, a plane – or a landing strip?

Erich von Däniken thought the lines might also be signals of some kind to alien beings. Others say that the drawings may have been made by the Nazca people to call the aliens back once they had left Earth.

Come back, Spaceman!

YOU DECIDE

Were the giant drawings in Peru made by humans – or by something out of this world? Only you can decide if the artists were aliens or ancients. Put your own lines down at the back of the book once you've made up your mind!

Crop Circles

OUR MISSION ...

... to work out who – or what – is making incredible patterns in fields of crops.

BURNING QUESTIONS

🔥 Can crop circles possibly be made by humans?
🔥 How and why are they made?
🔥 Are they the work of aliens?

MISSION DETAILS

Imagine you're a farmer. You grow wheat and your current crop is doing very nicely. You get up one morning and do the daily rounds – to discover the weirdest thing: a giant geometrical pattern in the middle of your field. It's very pretty – but not what you were expecting to see wiggling amongst your wheat.

This strange phenomenon has left farmers – and everyone else – scratching their heads in bewilderment. The crop circles, as they've become known, appear most years, come in many different designs, and look too good to have been made by a human in darkness. How – and why – does this happen?

THE LOCATION

Crop circles have been spotted in Britain for many years, but it wasn't until the 1970s and '80s that they began to get attention – because so many of them began appearing. Most of them were found in the countryside of southern England. The first one (actually there were three of them) that really made the news in Britain was discovered in Wiltshire in 1980. Since then Wiltshire has been famous for its crop-circle activity.

Crop circles have since appeared in many parts of England, including Kent, Sussex and Cornwall. But they have also been found around the world – in the USA, Canada, Europe, Australia and Japan. But, obviously, only in places where there are fields of crops . . .

crop circle found in Avebury, Wiltshire.

THE EVIDENCE

Crop circles are big news. People talk about them, visit them, take photos of them – there are even people who study them. They call themselves 'cerealogists'.

The circles can measure many metres in diameter and, like the Nazca Lines, they're best seen from the air. Their huge size raises more questions. As you know, it is really difficult to make a very large drawing on the ground, because you can't stand back and see exactly what you are doing. Whoever is making these patterns must be planning out the designs in a very skilful way. And as the circles are usually made at night, they must have brilliant night vision!

The crop circles themselves have evolved over time. They started off as simple circles but seem to become more detailed and impressive with every passing year. All kinds of shapes have been found, including rectangles, claws, and really complex designs of swirls, stars and spots. Symbols from ancient cultures have been found: there are webs, knots; even a complete diagram of a DNA structure! Many designs are based on complex mathematical and geometrical patterns. All of them are perfect and precise.

How Are They Made?

No one knows. But we do know that the crops – usually wheat, barley or rye – are pressed down flat against the ground to make the patterns.

57

- It's done with care – the crops are not cut down or damaged during the process
- Each circle or pattern is usually made in one direction, lying in either a clockwise or an anti-clockwise 'swirl'
- In some places the stalks are even beautifully woven together
- The circles usually appear from April to September – the growing seasons for crops and the best time to produce a distinctive pattern

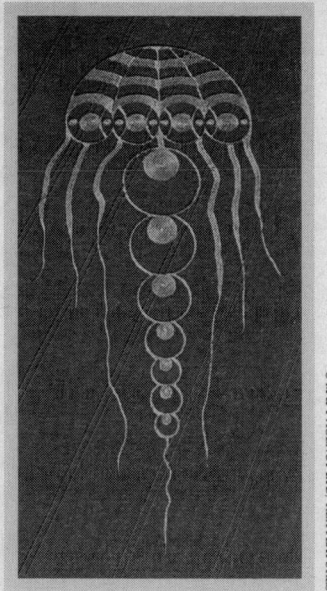

This pattern 'cropped' up in an Oxfordshire field in 2009. Something fishy about it?

A Message from Outer Space?

In 2001 two remarkable crop designs appeared close to a place called the Chilbolton Observatory in Hampshire. One showed a human face; the other was a pattern that looked like some kind of code.

Computer experts quickly realized that the message was in binary code – which is used as a way of encoding data for computers. Binary code is also one of the ways in which SETI – the Search for Extra-Terrestrial Intelligence (see page 95) – tries to communicate with possible aliens in the universe.

Back in 1974 SETI transmitted a message from a radio telescope – you can see it below. The message contained, among other things, information about the Earth's population, our solar system and the chemical elements that exist on Earth (as detailed on the middle diagram). It was directed at a star cluster called M13, which is about 25,000 light years away from us.

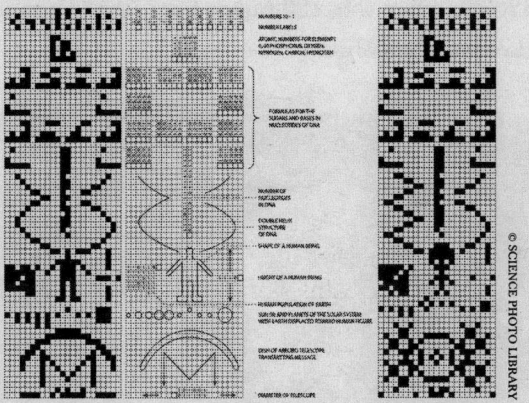

Take a look at the image on page 58 – taken from the crop circle. It looks very similar to the original message, doesn't it? In fact, it is an exact copy of the message sent by SETI, but with a few minor adjustments – for instance, 'silicon' has been added to the list of chemical elements.

Many people believe that this crop marking is a 'reply' message made by aliens! As aliens probably don't speak English very well, they have used the same binary code to reply to our original message, which was sent from Earth 27 years before. If this were true, it would be absolutely incredible – a letter from aliens! Made of wheat! An ET Wheat Meet!

However, before you get too excited, you should know that SETI – who take this sort of thing very seriously – were not impressed by the alien 'message'. They think that if an intelligent alien were trying to contact Earth, it would be way too advanced to be just making marks in fields.

But there's more. Things got even stranger the following year (2002), when this 120-metre-long image was found near Winchester, Hampshire:

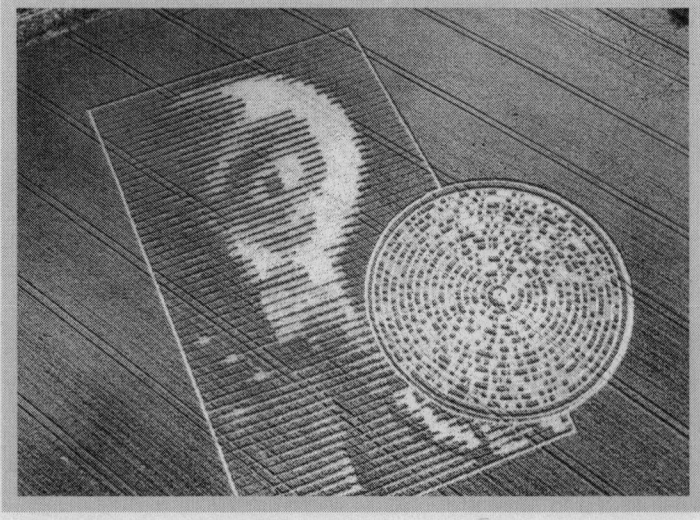

This amazing picture clearly shows the head of an alien, with three small shapes to the left which might be UFOs. A large circle containing symbols was decoded by researchers. The message appears to read:

Beware the bearers of FALSE gifts & their BROKEN PROMISES. Much PAIN but still time. [Damaged word.] There is GOOD out there. We OPpose DECEPTION. Conduit CLOSING (BELL SOUND).

Any idea what this means? Nope, me neither. The jury is split on this one. Many are convinced that this crop circle is some kind of weird letter from aliens (who sound really confused – maybe they're just learning English?), while others think it is all a hoax. Particularly as the alien 'face' looks like something from a bad TV show . . . So – what do you think?

MY MISSION

I could spend many, many nights camping out in fields to see if any crop-circle makers eventually turn up. Or I could try and see how difficult it really is to make a crop circle of my own. Because, let's face it, if I can do it, then anyone can!

Let me show you my crop-circle kit. I'm rather proud of it.

KIT LIST

 A PLANK OF WOOD – just over a metre long, with holes drilled in each end

 A LENGTH OF ROPE – about three metres long; each end of the rope needs to be put through the hole in the plank and securely knotted

 EXTRA-LONG MEASURING TAPES

 MARKERS – I'm using small bits of wood to stick in the ground

 NIGHT-VISION GOGGLES

A FRIEND TO HELP – you can't do this on your own

As this is my first attempt, I've kept it relatively simple – no jellyfish or alien faces for me. Just a large but perfect circle, with some smaller circles around the outside. I've done a sketch of my circles and have worked out how big they are going to be.

Now all I have to do is find a field and wait for a moonlit night . . .

MISSION COMPLETED

My crop circle turned out surprisingly well! I used a method called planking (which has nothing to do with the internet phenomenon of lying down like a plank in a public place; I'm simply using a plank in a public place).

Not this: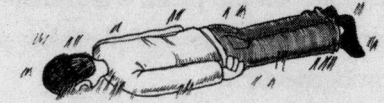

But this:

How to Make a Crop Circle

1. Find a public field with very long, straw-like grass. Farmers get a bit cross when you trample all over their livelihood, no matter how cool your pattern is!
2. Decide on the centre point of your circle and place a stake in the ground.
3. Get your helper/friend to stand on one end of the plank, to keep it still. This is the centre point of your circle.

4. The rope should be knotted through the plank holes. Loop the rope over your shoulders, with the plank on the ground in front of you. Put one foot on the plank, pressing down hard onto the ground. This flattens down the crops quite well.

5. Walk around your centre point in a complete circle while pressing down hard on the plank – and there you have it! A perfect, if small, crop circle. The plank has pressed down all the crops underneath it.

6. To make it bigger, all you need to do is to reposition your plank on the outside of the circle you have already made and walk around again. Each time you go around the circumference you will get a bigger circle – until it's massive!

So how did I manage to enter and leave the field without leaving any trace of my footsteps? No, not by levitating (now that would be impressive) but by walking on tractor tracks already made in the field so that no one could see where I had trodden. Clever!

Despite my success with a basic circle, I'm still struggling to see how the really complicated designs could be made, especially in the dead of night. Could a bunch of people with some planks of wood and pieces of rope really produce something as precise and fantastic as this?

Could this be achieved with an all-night planking marathon?

WHAT DO YOU THINK?

People have come up with all kinds of bizarre ideas to explain what causes crop circles, from hovering helicopters to rolling hedgehogs! Here are the four most likely explanations (no hedgehogs included):

1. Crop Circles Are Made by Wind

Could the patterns be caused by a natural force that is moving the crops around? Some people think so. They point to whirling winds called 'dust devils', which spin around madly, picking up lots of dust and dirt along the way. As all the tiny particles of dust whirl about, they bump into each other and produce an electric charge. Apparently some dust devils even give off a glowing light because of this electricity. Which would explain why unusual balls of lights have been seen moving in and around crop-circle fields.

But could a mini wind really carve out the incredibly complex designs that are sometimes found? And wouldn't these whirlwinds have been noticed by crop-circle investigators before now?

2. They Are Created by Natural Energy

A scientist called Dr Hans Jenny thinks the circles are caused by a different kind of 'natural' force – the force of sound. The idea is that vibrating sound frequencies could cause something solid – our crops – to be shaped into a geometric pattern.

Crop circles really get your head in a spin!

It's not as crazy as it sounds. Quite a few witnesses to crop circles claim to have heard a strange noise in the fields, usually before the circle appears. It's been described as a bit like a cicada (a kind of grasshopper) – a trilling sound. In the 1980s the noise was even recorded during the night by a group of researchers in England.

The recording was sent to the important-sounding NASA Jet Propulsion Laboratory in California. The experts there didn't think that it came from an insect or any other kind of creature – they said it was a mechanical noise and probably of 'intelligent' origin. You can draw your own conclusions from that – aliens or humans?

A fascinating experiment, performed in the 1960s, measured the effect of different kinds of music on the growth of plants. It found that:

- Thrashing heavy metal music made the plants bend away from the speakers – and sometimes die!
- Gentle classical music encouraged the plants to bend towards the music source

But there are other explanations for an unknown force of energy that could be behind the circles.

Mystical Lines
In the 1920s a man called Alfred Watkins discovered that certain ancient sites – such as standing stones, churches, forts and castles – could be connected by drawing invisible lines.

He named these 'ley lines'. He said that a ley line was a straight line connecting five sacred sites that were within five kilometres of each other.

Some people believe that ley lines are actually channels of energy that flow under the Earth's surface. They think that ancient civilizations knew all about them, which is why they built their special places on these pathways – to make the most of the Earth's energy at powerful points.

Could crop circles have some kind of connection with these invisible lines? Could energy from ley lines have something to do with the energy making the circles?

People have noticed that there are strange things going on in some of the circles, all connected to energy. Some say that mobile phones, compasses and other electrical devices don't work properly if they are inside the circles. One idea is that the energy in crop circles alters the electromagnetic field, affecting the working of the equipment.

Perhaps it's no coincidence that England has a large number of ancient sacred sites (therefore ley lines) – and also has the most crop circles?

Note: My top gardening tip – play relaxing music to your plants and flowers!

3. Crop Circles Are Hoaxes!

Could there be groups of crop-circle artists, creeping out at night to mystify and amaze the world with their designs? If this is true, then one thing's for sure: the circle hoaxers are not only brilliant at making circles – they're brilliant at keeping secrets. And so far, no one has ever 'grassed' on them!

So if the circles are secretly being made by humans, how are they doing it? Lots of people have tried to work this out. They've tried the same methods that I used to make my experimental circle – a simple kit involving wood and rope. Some have suggested that the hoaxers might use stools to move from one piece of the pattern to the other, which stops them from making too many giveaway marks in the crops.

A more recent idea has been suggested by a Professor Taylor from the University of Oregon. He thinks that the hoaxers are using gadgets called 'magnetrons' to make the patterns with. Ever heard of a magnetron? You could probably find one in your kitchen right now. It's a powerful tube found inside a microwave oven. It's the part that generates the microwaves, creating heat. The idea is that a creative person with a hand-held magnetron could flatten the crops much more easily than with a plank, and make really ambitious and complex circles – like some of the ones we've seen. Some researchers have even noted that a few crops show evidence of being blasted with microwave radiation.

One thing's for certain, though – some of the crop circles are definitely being made by humans. How do we know? They've admitted it . . .

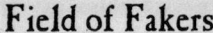

Field of Fakers

In 1991 two men, Doug Bower and Dave Chorley – known as Doug and Dave – confessed that since 1978 they had made hundreds of crop circles. They even made a film for the BBC demonstrating how they used planks, rope and wire to make their circles. Doug and Dave are said to have made more than 200 crop circles during their time as hoaxers.

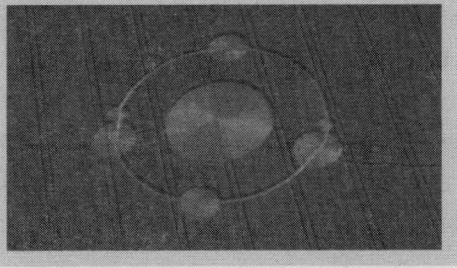

© JOZE POJBIC/ GETTY IMAGES

One of Doug and Dave's efforts. Not bad!

Other experiments have shown that humans can definitely make some impressive crop circles using simple equipment.

But even though this pair owned up to making their crop circles, does it mean that all the many hundreds of crop circles found around the world are hoaxes too? Perhaps it's a bit like UFOs – just because some of them are fakes doesn't mean all of them are . . .

4. Crop Circles Are Made by Aliens

Some people believe that the circles are the work of intelligent aliens. They think that the patterns may have been formed by alien landings, perhaps made by their spaceships hovering over the ground.

There are even witnesses who say they have seen strange glowing balls of light and heard inexplicable noises – high-pitched sounds and strange crackling – around the fields when the crop circles are found (possibly ball lightning? – see page 18). One person thought they saw a tube of light coming down from the skies and making the pattern.

In Wiltshire in the summer of 2009, a policeman approached three tall mysterious blond-haired figures standing close to a crop circle that had appeared a few days earlier. There was a weird crackling sound and he said that the plants appeared to be moving. As the policeman got closer, the three figures ran away 'faster than any man he had ever seen'. Could they have been humans – or something from out of this world?

There is also the question of the mysterious patterns, which some think are coded messages left by aliens. The best examples of these are the 2001/2002 crop faces and signs found in Hampshire (page 60).

If this is the case, what exactly are the aliens trying to communicate to us? Look back at the 'message' on page 60. Perhaps making a circle is their way of saying 'hello'? Or maybe they just really enjoy making artistic patterns in our fields – using planet Earth as a canvas for their creative ideas?

YOU DECIDE

Crop circles are definitely one of the most perplexing mysteries around. And no one has managed to come up with a satisfactory answer. Is it all a conspiracy, or are creatures from another planet responsible? It's up to you!

The
Existence of Aliens

THE MISSION...

... to find out if there are aliens anywhere in our universe ...

BURNING QUESTIONS

- Is there life on other planets or moons?
- What would a real alien look like?
- How can we find an alien?

MISSION DETAILS

As mysteries go, this is a biggie. Perhaps the biggest of all time? Is there life 'out there'?

Humans have always gazed up at the stars and planets, wondering if there are other worlds up there – and what kinds of creatures might be living on them. Would they be anything like us – or completely 'out of this world'?

But even though we are getting to know much more about our solar system, and what lies beyond it, we're really none

the wiser. And if aliens *do* exist, are they responsible for all the weird stuff we've investigated in this book, like UFOs and crop circles?

My mission is to search out aliens – but there's one big problem. The size of the search area . . .

THE LOCATION

Ever heard the expression 'looking for a needle in a haystack'? It pretty much sums up our problem. The universe is the biggest thing you can possibly imagine. Actually it's so big, you *can't* imagine it. Words like 'massive', 'immense', even 'humongous' (is that a real word?) just don't do the job.

To make things even more mindboggling, scientists believe that the universe is getting even bigger. It's expanding as you're reading this book! (Though I'm not quite sure *how* scientists know this – they must have such long tape measures . . .)

To get an idea of the scale of things:

- Our planet, Earth, is one of eight planets currently orbiting the Sun, our star. This is our solar system. Huge!
- But it's only one of many, many solar systems. All these solar systems together make up a galaxy. Our galaxy is called the Milky Way
- And it doesn't stop there. Astronomers think there may be billions of other galaxies out there, each with its own group of solar systems! It's all too much for my little brain to cope with . . .

All these galaxies, along with all the other stuff in space – like meteorites, comets, dust and gas – make up the universe. So we have our location. But where in the universe do we start?

THE EVIDENCE

Aliens are everywhere! In books, stories, movies and TV programmes, there's no shortage of little green men, man-eating monsters and cuddly extra-terrestrials.

Humans are fascinated – and terrified – by the idea of aliens (I'm not too proud to admit that I still hide behind the sofa when *Doctor Who* is on). And it's no surprise, with so many scary movies and TV shows around. Who wouldn't be nervous about the idea of unfriendly aliens arriving in flying saucers, desperate to get their claws on Earth? More 'extra-terror-estrials' than cuddly ETs?!

But, scary or not, how far have we got in our real-life search for aliens?

Note: By the way, 'extra-terrestrial' is a Latin phrase meaning anything that comes from outside Earth. But it is often used to mean 'alien' – especially when shortened to ET. *ET* is also the name of a famous movie about a cute and cuddly alien who gets stranded on planet Earth and needs to phone home. You've probably seen it. . .

The Age of Space Travel

Up until the 1950s and '60s we'd been able to observe space – but never to reach it ourselves. Everything changed with technology. In 1957 the very first human-made satellite, *Sputnik 1,* was sent into space by the Russians. From then on, space was big news. The Americans and Russians got really competitive with each other to see who could complete each space 'first' – things like:

- The first living creature in space (a dog called Laika in 1957 – that was the Russians)
- The first person to orbit the Earth (Yuri Gagarin in 1961 – the Russians again)
- And the biggie – the first human to set foot on the Moon (this time the Americans won)

The 1969 trip to the Moon was probably the most incredible event that has ever happened in our history. Think about it – for the first time ever, a human set foot on another world! Millions of people watched as astronaut Neil Armstrong stepped onto the Moon's surface, uttering the famous words, *'That's one small step for man, one giant leap for mankind . . .'*

Proud Neil flies the flag for the good old USA.

So, did Neil and his space companion, Buzz Aldrin, find any ETs on the moon? Nope: going to the Moon proved once and for all that there was a disappointing lack of aliens living on our closest 'heavenly body'.

Meanwhile, back on 1960s Earth, Neil's moonwalk had made space the coolest thing ever. Kids were pretending to be astronauts, just like him. Space toys were the number one Christmas present. People were reading science fiction comics and watching great new TV shows like *Star Trek* and *Doctor Who*. All featured thrilling space adventures and a bizarre collection of aliens (which looked like they'd been made out of toilet rolls and cling film, but no one seemed to care).

People started going out to watch sci-fi movies at their local cinema. These films seemed to have one thing in common – scaring the living daylights out of the public. Movies like:

- 🌎 *Invasion of the Body Snatchers* – aliens invade Earth by taking over the bodies of humans, one by one. Spooky . . .
- 🌎 *The Day of the Triffids* – weird alien plants (called Triffids) try to take over our planet. Doesn't sound possible, but these are plants are killers – and they can 'walk'. Eeek!
- 🌎 *The Blob* – when a meteorite lands on Earth, a jelly-like blob emerges. Sounds harmless, but it soon grows, then starts eating humans . . .

But the thing is, despite all these fantastic – and horrible – aliens we've invented, we actually have *no idea* what a real alien would look like.

Here on Earth, creatures have evolved to suit all the many different environments in our world, and we have thousands of different species on our planet.

Think about it: if other planets had a similar number of different species, suited to their very different environments, the possibilities are endless! Aliens might look nothing like what we've imagined.

Whatever we find, we'll just have to hope that real aliens aren't as scary as the ones we've made up in movies!

Alien Abduction

Plenty of people think they've seen a UFO or an alien, or even both. Some even believe that they have been kidnapped by aliens and taken on board their spaceship.

Take, for example, Travis Walton, a logger from Arizona, USA. At the end of a long day in November 1975, he and six colleagues were driving home at dusk when a bright light in the distance caught their attention. It seemed to be coming from a strange silver disc, about six metres in diameter and hovering in the air, wobbling from side to side. The men had never seen anything like it before, and Travis (who was either very brave or very foolish – you decide) thought he would investigate. As he got closer to the UFO, his friends saw a beam of bluish-green light whoosh out of it and strike his body. Poor old Travis was jolted upwards into the air, and he landed, outstretched and unconscious, on the ground. His (less brave) friends quickly drove off, convinced he was dead, and terrified that the same thing would happen to them. When they'd calmed down, they drove back to the same spot – but there was no sign of Travis or the weird disc.

The police were called and an extensive search took place for the missing man, but nothing was found. It was a mystery. What on earth had happened to Travis Walton?

Five days later, Travis appeared at a local petrol station in a nervous, panic-stricken state. His story?

Travis said he had been abducted by aliens and held in their spaceship. The aliens he described were short and bald, with big heads and large staring eyes. Travis was so terrified to find the aliens looking at him that he passed out – then found himself at the petrol station when he woke up. He had been missing for five 'Earth' days, yet he was convinced that he had only been gone for a few hours. This kind of 'time-slip' crops up quite often in reports of alien encounters.

Travis Walton's experience remains one of the most talked-about alien mysteries, and his story was later made into a book and film. Some think that, because there were seven witnesses to the UFO, the story must be true; others think that the whole thing was a big hoax, made up by Travis and his friends.

Whether you believe him or not, his description of the aliens does fit that of others who say they have seen ETs. People like Betty and Barney Hill, who say that in September 1961 they were followed in their car by an alien spacecraft. They then 'lost' two hours of time. The couple later remembered being taken up into the craft and meeting aliens.

Travis Walton – innocent victim of aliens or hoaxer?

Betty says that she even asked one of the aliens where it had come from and that he showed her a map of the stars. Good to know that you can always rely on an ET to help you with directions . . .

The aliens that the Hills and Travis Walton encountered are now officially known as Grey Aliens – the most common description given by those who say they've seen one.

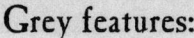

Grey features:

- 🌑 The size of a small human – 1.5 metres
- 🌑 Large black eyes
- 🌑 Small nose and mouth
- 🌑 Large head
- 🌑 Pale grey skin
- 🌑 Smooth and hairless

Have you seen this alien?

Could this really be what an alien looks like, or were our 'witnesses' imagining things? And whether a real-life alien is grey, blue or green, how – and where – will we find them?

The Search for Life

Finding an alien isn't as simple as getting into a rocket and jetting off into the stratosphere. Manned missions – that's missions with humans on board – are incredibly difficult to organize and cost billions of pounds. They can also be very risky for the astronauts who take part in them. I mean, would you fancy being blasted through Earth's atmosphere in a rocket to the unknown? Added to the 'challenging' journey are other risks, including:

- 🌑 High levels of dangerous radiation in deep space
- 🌑 Violent solar storms
- 🌑 And, if anything goes wrong on your mission, no one is going to be able to rescue you . . .

If you think about it, astronauts are *really, really* brave!

A less risky – and cheaper – way of finding out about other planets is to send unmanned probes. These are specially designed robotic craft which can travel to and land on distant planets, making fantastically long journeys that humans could not survive. These robotic probes can take photographs, pick up soil and rock samples – even whip up a quick spag Bol (I'm joking). In this way we've been able to find out lots more about other places where ETs might be discovered.

A sky crane lands the rover Curiosity on the planet Mars in 2012.

So far, we've landed probes on planets like Venus and Mars, and explored several different moons looking for evidence of life. Missions such as *Voyager*, *Galileo* and *Magellan* have brought us information about places we can only dream of visiting ourselves.

What are we looking for?

It's quite simple, really. To find life, we really need to find a planet that's like ours – good old planet Earth.

Why? Because our planet has been mega-successful when it comes to creating life. Earth has the most amazing variety and number of different life forms, so it makes sense for scientists to look for other planets that have similar conditions to ours.

What life needs

- **Wonderful water**: Life here on Earth probably began in water. And nothing can survive on our planet without it. Luckily, research has revealed that liquid water is pretty common in our solar system. Probes have found evidence of the existence of water on Mars and Europa (one of Jupiter's moons); on the planet Venus; and also on Titan and Enceladus (both moons of Saturn), and Ganymede and Callisto (both moons of Europa)

- **Creative carbon**: Did you know that you are a carbon-based life form? You do now! Every cell of every living thing on our planet contains carbon

Carbon is a crucial part of what makes life happen. It is an element that combines with other elements – hydrogen, nitrogen and oxygen – to make the complex chemicals that life needs. And there's a lot of carbon out there in space – because it is made by stars!

All living things that we know of need carbon, but some scientists think it might be possible for an alien life form to be based on another element. Some think that silicon could be that element. If that happened, no one knows what the results would be like. Sci-fi writers have imagined all kinds of weird silicon-based life forms: in his story *A Martian Odyssey*, Stanley Weisbaum described a slow-moving creature, over half a million years old, which poos silicon bricks. Ouch!

An artist imagines a silicon life form created from crystals. Or is it a giant prawn?

🌑 **The right light**: Living creatures need sunlight for energy and warmth. Earth lies in what's been nicknamed the 'Goldilocks Zone' – in just the right position. It isn't too close to our sun – if it was, it would be so hot, all our water would evaporate (and we'd be finished). But it isn't too far away from the Sun either – if it was, it would be too cold, dark and frozen for anything to survive

Like Baby Bear's porridge, Earth is 'just right' when it comes to being the perfect distance from our sun, and the perfect temperature for life to thrive.

Here are a few places in our solar system that we are currently exploring to see if the conditions are right for life:

Is there life on Mars?

We call Mars the Red Planet because it is covered in iron oxide – aka rust. Mars is smaller, colder and drier than Earth, but even so, there are hopes for finding life here one day. NASA have so far made seven landings on Mars with robotic probes – the latest was *Curiosity* (great name) in August 2012.

Most importantly, there is water on Mars – though most of it is frozen in Mars's ice caps, because it's so cold there. Scientists think that Mars was once much warmer, so if the water was liquid in the past, life of some kind could have existed. The surface of the Red Planet shows that it may once have had seas and rivers.

Nowadays it is probably too cold and dry for anything to be living on the surface, though scientists think there might still be something underground – perhaps bacteria or simple life forms. Even that would be a major breakthrough, because bacteria are the basic beginnings of all life, even here on Earth. The earliest evidence for life on our planet has been found in Australia – in 3.4-billion-year-old mats of bacteria called stromatolites. So if scientists can find bacteria on other planets, it tells us that the potential for many more life forms to evolve is there.

The search continues – and even though the journey to Mars would be extraordinarily difficult for humans to manage, scientists are trying to find a way to make it possible.

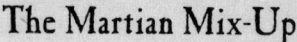

The Martian Mix-Up

People have long thought that there were aliens living on Mars – not because of science but because of a language mistake.

Back in 1877, an Italian astronomer called Schiaparelli announced that he'd spotted some interesting things on the surface of the planet Mars – long vertical lines that he called 'canali'.

I can speak a little Italian, you know: *pizza, pasta, panini* … I'm practically bi-lingual. Sadly, many people aren't as gifted as 'moi' (French – just testing) when it comes to languages. So there was a slight problem over the word 'canali': the English thought it meant 'canal', though it actually means 'channel' in Italian. What's the difference? Channels can occur naturally, while canals are most definitely made – by someone – or something …

An astronomer called Percival Lowell heard about the 'canali' and got very excited. He reasoned that if there were canals on Mars, there must be intelligent beings living there who had built the canals. The idea soon got around and a name was coined for the Mars-dwelling creatures – Martians!

There was no evidence for this – but the idea of Martians caught people's imaginations. Ever heard of *War of the Worlds* by H. G. Wells? In this famous book, Wells created a frightening vision of the future where alien machines from Mars landed on Earth and started to destroy everything in sight.

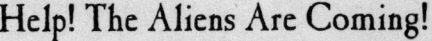

Help! The Aliens Are Coming!

Amazingly, the hysterical crowd scenes described by H. G. Wells in his fictional story actually happened in real life in the USA. In 1938 famous director Orson Welles made a radio play of *War of the Worlds* – with disastrous results. The actors in the play were so convincing that many listeners thought that it was a real-time news broadcast. Believing that Martians were invading Earth, panicking crowds fled their homes! Maybe they thought the Martians were looking for food – perhaps Mars bars, mars-malade or mars-mallows??

Chaotic crowds learn never to compete with a Martian in a three-legged race!

In real life, Martians may not turn out to be anything like the tripods of H. G. Wells's famous book – but wouldn't it be just a-mars-ing to find life on the Red Planet?

More Homes for Aliens?

Lying beyond the Earth and Mars are the two giant gas planets, Jupiter and Saturn. There's not much chance of anything living in these freezing places as their atmospheres are full of poisonous gases. But both have a number of moons orbiting them – and these moons have totally surprised scientists with their possibilities.

Incredible Europa

One place that scientists are really excited about is Europa, one of the moons of the planet Jupiter. You might not have heard of it, but Europa was discovered a long time ago, in 1610, by Italian astronomer Galileo Galilei.

Too clever for their times?

Imagine living hundreds of years ago, long before the telescope was invented. You can see the Sun and the Moon but you don't know anything scientific about the universe. Would you have believed that the Earth was at the centre of everything – and that all the planets and everything else revolved around our world? Most people did. Wrongly, of course!

It wasn't until 1514 that a Polish astronomer called Copernicus came up with a big, big idea. He published a book saying that he believed that the Earth moved around the Sun.

This shocking revelation was just too much for people in the sixteenth century – especially those in charge, who really didn't like their ideas being challenged. Poor old Copernicus's book was trashed. He probably would have gone to jail (these were harsh times) but he died soon afterwards.

In the 1600s, however, an Italian physicist, mathematician and all-round brainiac called Galileo used a proper telescope for the first time. Galileo discovered all sorts of amazing things about the planets and moons, and declared that

Copernicus had been right all along (and he had!). For this Galileo was sentenced to life imprisonment, in 1633.

If either of them had been born in different times, they might have been as respected and admired as, say, Professor Stephen Hawking is today. Life can be very unfair. . .

Images from probes have shown large areas of water on Europa's surface, which are probably huge oceans or lakes. It's unbelievably cold on Europa – a freezing -160° C on the surface – so it is covered in a thick crust of ice, between three and seven kilometres thick (that's thick – if there is life on Europa, they could ice skate without worrying. . . !). But experts believe that warmer waters lie underneath the crust.

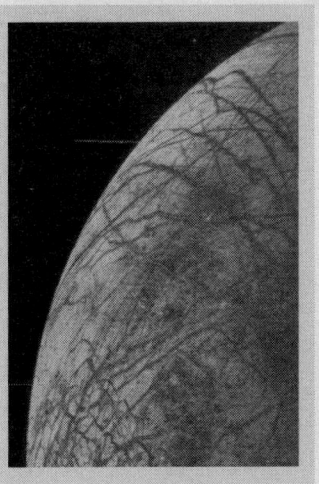

This is how icy Europa might look when lit by the Sun.

This is because the massive gravitational pull of Jupiter creates enough heat to warm up Europa's interior, but not quite enough to melt the icy crust on top. This fact, along with the discovery of some fascinating new creatures on Earth, has made scientists think that Europa's waters may hold some very interesting finds.

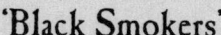

'Black Smokers'

Deep down in some of Earth's oceans are smoking black plumes called hydrothermal vents. They happen when cold sea water on the sea floor meets hot magma bubbling up from below the Earth's surface. When the hot fluid bursts through a crack into the sea water, you've got yourself a hydrothermal vent. Also known as a 'black smoker'.

I said earlier that all life needs sunlight to survive. But it turns out the experts weren't quite accurate (yes, even boffins are sometimes wrong). No one thought that life could possibly exist at the very bottom of the sea, where no sunlight can penetrate. But we recently discovered that not only are there bacteria, shrimp and crabs in the darkest depths, there is a weird new creature on the black-smoker block – the tube worm.

Scientists have found lots of red and white tube-shaped creatures, about a metre long, which are completely blind and have no mouth (very attractive!). More incredibly, this new species has found a way to survive without any light at all – something we just didn't believe was possible. Clearly scientists don't have all the answers!

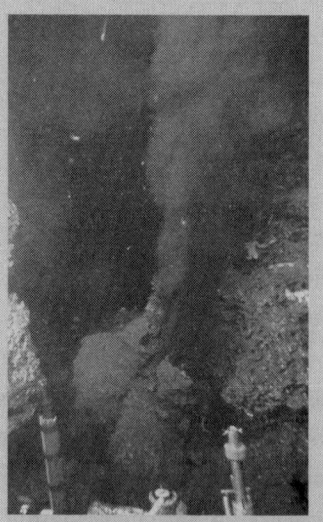

© DR KEN MACDONALD/ SCIENCE PHOTO LIBRARY

These vents are smokin'!

Experts think that Europa could possibly have hydrothermal vents, like Earth. If so, could alien creatures be living deep in its waters, around the vents? Something even weirder than a blind, mouthless tube worm maybe . . .

To find out for sure, a mission to Europa would need to land, penetrate the massively thick icy crust, explore the deep waters, and somehow bring any life forms back to Earth – but where there's a will . . .

Life Is Tough

Everywhere we look on our planet, life is flourishing – even in places where we once thought it was impossible. In recent years, scientists have found life forms alive and well in some very unusual places, not just the oceans. Like the driest desert in the world (the Atacama in Chile) and the freezing ice of Antarctica.

These tough species are called 'extremophiles' – things that can survive in extreme environments in which no normal life form would have a chance.

The existence of extremophiles has made the chances of finding life on other planets even better. Because now scientists know that life might be able to begin and survive on other worlds that have hostile environments.

More missions are being planned for the 2020s – to Europa, and to Jupiter's other moons – which will hopefully tell us more.

Terrific Titan

Titan is the largest moon of the planet Saturn. Scientists are excited about Titan because it is a bit like Earth was many years ago. It has nitrogen, like Earth, and is covered in mountains, lakes and river beds. It is much, much colder, though, and there is no liquid water, which is a big problem. Or is it?

In 2005 the *Cassini-Huygens* space probe finally reached Titan after a seven-year journey. It sent back pictures of oceans, made not of water but of liquid methane. Scientists have been thinking about an exciting possibility for Titan: could alien creatures have evolved that use liquid methane to live rather than water? They might look and behave in a completely different way to us Earthlings, because they would have developed using a different chemical structure. Mind-blowing . . .

The probe also told us that hydrogen gas detected in Titan's atmosphere seems to be flowing down and disappearing at its surface. One reason for this could be that the hydrogen is being used up – breathed – by alien life forms.

Moons, Planets and Stars . . .

OK – with all this talk of moons, I have to admit, before I started on this mission I wasn't really sure what the difference was between a planet, a moon and a star. Here's some help in case you don't know either (go on, admit it):

- A star is a huge, hot burning ball of gas, which makes energy and light. Our sun, for example

- A planet orbits a star. It can be rocky, like Earth, or a gas giant like Jupiter. It doesn't burn but is illuminated by light from its star

- A moon orbits a planet. Some planets have many moons – so far, 63 moons have been counted orbiting Jupiter. That makes our single Earth moon seem a little bit sad, doesn't it . . .

In our solar system we have a total of eight planets. Here they are in order of distance from the Sun (starting with the closest): Mercury, Venus, Earth, Mars, Jupiter, Saturn, Uranus and Neptune.

If you look at older books or websites, you may read that our solar system has nine planets – that's because Pluto got 'downgraded' in 2006. In other words, it was kicked out of the solar system by scientists. Poor old Pluto!

Far, Far Away . . .

So we've looked at aliens that might be found within our solar system – but what about even further afield?

In 1995 the very first planet outside our solar system was discovered. It is orbiting a star called 51 Peg. Since then we've gone on to discover many more distant planets with an incredible piece of technology . . .

The Kepler Telescope

In 2009 a gigantic space telescope was launched into space by NASA, the US space agency. Its mission? To find Earth-like planets outside our solar system. The Kepler Telescope is currently observing about 100,000 stars.

How does it find new planets? This amazing telescope looks at changes in the brightness of stars. A dip in a star's light could mean that an orbiting planet has just moved across its face.

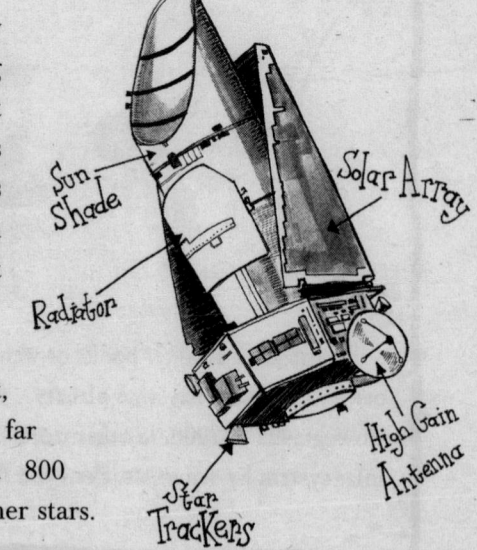

Sun Shade

Solar Array

Radiator

High Gain Antenna

Star Trackers

Using this equipment, astronomers have so far discovered more than 800 new planets orbiting other stars.

These strange new worlds are called exoplanets. So far we've discovered that:

- About 54 of these exoplanets are of a similar size to Earth
- They also happen to be in their 'Goldilocks Zone' – just the right distance from their sun

But this is just the tip of the exoplanet iceberg. There might be many, many more of them. But because these planets are in other solar systems, the distances involved are incredible. Even sending unmanned probes to an exoplanet would be a marathon task.

How can we find life if it is so far away?

The Alien Hunters

Some people really do have dream jobs – chocolate taster, waterslide tester, computer-game designer all spring to mind. But one of the coolest jobs of all has got to be that of 'alien hunter'. Which is exactly what the people at SETI do.

A houseful of alien hunters . . .

So what is SETI exactly? The word stands for the Search for Extra-Terrestrial Intelligence – an organization set up in 1984. The people who work for SETI have one aim –

to find signs of intelligent alien life. They are looking for thinking, feeling beings who can properly communicate with us.

They do this, not by zipping up a space suit and blasting off into the stratospherespace, but by using advanced technology to try and detect signals made by intelligent life forms.

SETI are currently scanning the stars, looking for radio and laser transmissions from distant civilizations in far-off solar systems. To do this, they need top-notch technology: roll out some more great gadgets . . .

The All-Sky SETI Optical Telescope – (OSETI)

This impressive telescope was launched in 2006 and scans the night sky with a huge 72-inch mirror, looking for laser signals that might be transmitted by distant extra-terrestrials. This tasty bit of kit can apparently process one terabit (a trillion bits!) of data – that's as much data as in all the books in the world – every second! So it should be able to cope with whatever our intelligent aliens might throw at it.

Listening to the skies

Perched in the Californian desert are a row of radio telescopes that look like giant dishes. Their job is to detect 'noise'; specifically noise that might be coming from other civilizations.

© THE PLANETARY SOCIETY

Not an easy job, given that there is so much other noise around us, like man-made signals from our TV stations, radar and satellites.

The Allen Telescope Array (for that is what they are called) listens out for narrow-bandwidth radio signals coming from outside the solar system. Because these signals don't occur naturally, finding one would mean that something intelligent must have made it.

The Allen Telescope Array on their noise-busting mission.

What they want to find is called a 'beacon' — a clear and definite signal that has been sent by intelligent aliens who are trying to communicate with us.

WOW!!

Has a beacon signal ever been found? Maybe!

In the summer of 1977 a radio telescope in Ohio, USA, picked up an incredibly exciting signal. So exciting that the astronomer on duty wrote *WOW!* on the printout when he spotted it.

Incredibly, it's been known as the WOW signal ever since.

The signal was coming from somewhere near the constellation Sagittarius, and appeared as a series of numbers and letters on the printout (so not an actual sound).

SETI thinks that it was not made by anything human and that it could have come from intelligent aliens with a very powerful transmitter. The signal has never been repeated – but the alien hunters at SETI are ready and waiting for the next one to come along.

Some even think that aliens might have been listening in to accidental signals from Earth for a long time. Our planet began transmitting radio and television signals about 100 years ago, and some of these transmissions will have leaked into space. A faraway alien might be picking up those signals right now. Let's just hope they haven't tuned in to more reruns of *Come Dine with Me* . . .

Message in a Space Bottle

So if aliens are trying to communicate with us, are we doing them the same favour? Well, kind of. Back in the 1970s, messages to aliens were placed on board the *Voyager* and *Pioneer* probes. They've now been travelling for more than 30 years and no one knows exactly where they are, or if an alien has picked them up. So what exactly have we put in our space-age 'message in a bottle'?

The two *Pioneer* probes have gold-coloured plaques on their sides, showing the date the mission left and the location of Earth in the universe. They also have illustrations of a man and woman on them, who are supposed to be everyday Earthlings. The man is waving in a friendly way – hopefully, showing the aliens that we humans come in peace, even though some of us have forgotten to put any clothes on

Maybe an alien is scratching its head over this picture at this very moment!

On board *Voyager* are some vinyl records (which we once used to play music – just ask a grown-up). Fortunately, full instructions for playing the records are also included, just in case aliens aren't familiar with ancient Earth rituals

The records contain different sounds from the Earth: laughter, heartbeats, footsteps, a volcano, thunder, the wind, rain and sea – even the sound of a chimpanzee! (This could be very confusing for an alien – it might think that all we Earth dwellers do is monkey around . . .)

There are greetings in 55 different languages, and pictures of humans, animals, plants and buildings. There's music too. We're not sure who made the selection, but it includes Beethoven and a blues singer called Blind Willie Johnson.

Voyager is now known to be at the outer limits of our solar system and it holds the record for being the most distant human-made object in the universe. Bet Blind Willie never thought he would get so far with his music!

MY MISSION

Going on a space mission would quite literally be 'a blast'. But, much as I would love to zoom off into the galaxy in search of aliens, it's just not possible – yet. One of the biggest problems is time.

Take a trip to Mars, for example. There's a very good reason why we haven't sent any human astronauts there. The total journey time from Earth to Mars would be up to a whopping 300 days, depending on the position of Earth and Mars at that time (remember, both planets are constantly in orbit).

So nearly a year to get there – then you'll need to spend some time on the Red Planet – and then get back to Earth again. That's a very long time to be in a spacecraft. Long enough to drive you a bit crazy – you might come back an 'astro*nut*' rather than an astronaut!

Despite the time issue, space experts are working hard on a

way of getting humans safely to the Red Planet – which will, hopefully, be in your lifetime. Maybe one day you'll be the first person to set foot on Mars!

If you are that person, this is what you'll need to take along:

KIT LIST

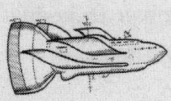 A MEGA MARS SPACECRAFT – it doesn't exist yet, but when it does, it will need to carry a huge amount of stuff (the technical term is 'payload'). Enough oxygen, food, water and fuel for a two-year trip – it will be the heaviest spacecraft ever . . .

 ENTERTAINMENT – to make the two years a bit more bearable, you'll want a selection of movies, games and music to while away the hours

 PRESSURIZED SPACE SUIT AND HELMET – when you leave the craft to explore, you'll need this specially designed suit to withstand the freezing Martian temperatures and the incredible amount of dust on the Red Planet

 MECHANICAL GRABBER – this special tool retrieves and collects objects – because your gloved fingers will be about as useful as a packet of sausages

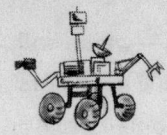 **ROBOTIC ROVER ASSISTANT** – to carry your air supply, communications system, tools and generator

 **SPACE TOOLS** – to probe the surface, you will need a specialist axe, hammer and a corer (for taking soil samples)

 **BACKPACK** – contains enough power to keep you alive for eight hours once off the craft

© POPULAR SCIENCE VIA GETTY IMAGES

Here, boy! A robotic rover in action – every astronaut's best friend.

MISSION COMPLETED

For the moment, the nearest I'm going to get to outer space is a visit to my local science museum. But I could make up for it by planning a very different type of holiday . . .

The First Ever 'Space Vacation'
Sometime in the next few years, a Virgin Galactic spacecraft will blast off from Earth at speeds of up to 4,000 kph. Passengers will experience what it is really like to travel into outer space and will get an incredible view of Earth from above. Awesome!

They'll be travelling in a rocket-powered space plane, which will be launched from an aircraft at around 50,000 feet, just above the Earth's atmosphere. The journey will be short but fun – passengers will float and spin around as they experience micro-gravity!

But I'd better start saving up. It won't be cheap – but many would say it was worth it for the ultimate trip of a lifetime. For now, I'll just put my name on the waiting list . . .

WHAT DO YOU THINK?

1. Aliens Do Exist
Do you believe that we are not alone in the universe? Many astronomers would agree with you. This is why:

Sheer Numbers
It's all a numbers game. There's a well-known saying:

'Give enough monkeys enough typewriters, and one of them will write Shakespeare.' The planetary argument is similar. There are just *so many* planets out there. Scientists think that there are billions of them in just our galaxy, the Milky Way. And there are billions more galaxies, each with billions of stars!

Some experts think that at least half of these stars will have planets orbiting them. And the chances are that some of the planets will be similar to Earth and will have developed life forms.

Unfortunately, it would take so long for a human to travel to another solar system that we'd be dead years before we arrived at our destination. So we'll keep relying on even more advanced space probes and telescopes to do the faraway investigating for us.

Perhaps one day SETI will pick up a clear and direct message from an alien in a distant solar system. Maybe aliens are watching us right now – and laughing at our primitive inventions!

Thoughts of a Space Genius

I'm no space geek. I used to think black holes were something you found in black socks. So let's find out what a real space expert thinks about aliens.

Welcome, Professor Stephen Hawking. He's the famous astrophysicist who blows people's minds with his incredible

ideas – such as the real possibility of time travel. He knows pretty much everything a human can possibly know about the universe and has written lots of amazing books about the subject.

So, what does Prof Hawking think about aliens? To put it simply, he doesn't believe that we are the only life form in the universe. He once said:

'To my mathematical brain, the numbers alone make thinking about aliens perfectly rational ... The real challenge is to work out what aliens might actually be like.'

This view is backed up by the super-brainy scientists at SETI. Who, of course, wouldn't be spending all their valuable time searching for alien signals if they didn't truly believe that intelligent life could exist in the universe. As SETI say: *'Given a suitable environment and sufficient time, life will develop on other planets.'* Evidence enough?

2. Aliens Don't Exist

Perhaps you're one of these people who don't believe anything unless you see it with your own eyes? And the chances are you've not come across an alien yet. (Though if you ever do encounter a real-life ET, please do let me know.)

To date, not a single person, not even an astronaut – or Stephen Hawking, for that matter – has come up with a proper recording of an alien, or a photograph, or any other hard evidence. There are thousands of stories, reports and cases, but all of them could be put down to hoaxes or genuine mistakes.

And if aliens and UFOs were visiting us on a regular basis, as so many seem to believe, why would they be so shy about making themselves known to us humans? Why send garbled messages in code or make weird lines and circles on Earth's surface? And why would we still not have any proper evidence, like a captured UFO?

There's certainly a lot of nonsense talked about aliens. And many scientists don't believe that any of the weird monsters that appear in movies like *Men in Black* will bear any resemblance to real aliens.

The kind of ET normally seen in films – but would they be anything like real-life aliens?

It's true that many space experts believe that alien life forms of some kind do exist. But maybe – like the scientists who thought that life couldn't exist without sunlight – they're just wrong? Really, the only way to prove aliens exist is to find one!

YOU DECIDE

Do aliens exist or not? It's 'make your mind up' time. So head to the back of the book to make your notes! The answer is out there – somewhere. In the meantime, we'll keep on looking . . .

WANT TO KNOW MORE?

George's Secret Key to the Universe, George's Cosmic Treasure Hunt, George and the Big Bang, George and the Unbreakable Code – Lucy and Stephen Hawking (Corgi)

The Alien Hunter's Handbook – Mark Brake (Kingfisher)

Monster Tracker: The Alien Hunter's Guide – Gomer Bolstrood (Watts)

Can Science Solve? The Mystery of UFOs – Chris Oxlade (Heinemann)

The Twilight Realm: Aliens – Jim Pipe (Wayland)

Ask Uncle Albert: 100½ Tricky Science Questions Answered – Russell Stannard (Faber & Faber)

www.nasa.gov

NASA for kids – **www.nasa.gov/audience/forkids/kidsclub**

www.nationalgeographic.com

www.planetary.org/explore/for-kids/

DECISION TIME

So, we've looked at the evidence (which sometimes got a bit too close for comfort, if you ask me). Now it's time for you to sort the facts from the fiction and solve some of the world's greatest mysteries once and for all . . .

Mystery 1: The UFO Enigma

Notes:

_____

_____

_____

_____

Possible explanations:

☐ 1. *UFOs Are Sent by Aliens*

☐ 2. *UFOs Are All Explainable*

☐ 3. *Other* _____

Mystery 2: The Roswell Incident

Notes:

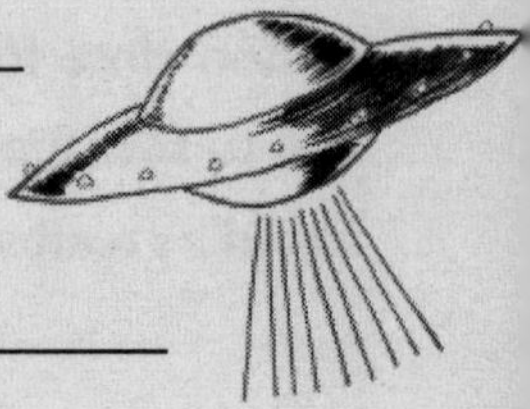

_____

_____

_____

_____

Possible explanations:

☐ *1. The Object Was an Alien Spaceship*

☐ *2. The Object Was a Spy Balloon*

☐ *3. Other* _____

Mystery 3: The Nazca Lines

Notes:

_____

_____

_____

_____

☐ *1. The Nazca Lines Were Made by Humans*

☐ *2. The Lines Were Made by Aliens*

☐ *3. Other* _____

Mystery 4: Crop Circles

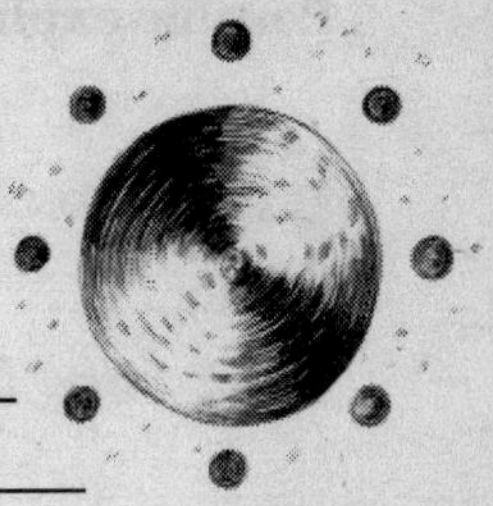

Notes:

_____

_____

_____

_____

Possible explanations:

☐ *1. Crop Circles Are Made by Wind*

☐ *2. They Are Created by Natural Energy*

☐ *3. Crop Circles Are Hoaxes!*

☐ *4. Crop Circles Are Made by Aliens*

☐ *5. Other* _____

Mystery 5: The Existence of Aliens

Notes:

_____

_____

_____

_____

Possible explanations:

☐ *1. Aliens Do Exist* _____

☐ *2 Aliens Don't Exist* _____

☐ *3. Other* _____

If you enjoyed this book, why not try
the other titles in the series?

GREAT MYSTERIES OF THE WORLD

ANCIENT TREASURES
CREEPY CREATURES
WEIRD WATERS

Read every out-of-this-world adventure!

Take a ride through space and discover the mysteries of science and the universe with George and a super-intelligent computer called Cosmos.

But someone else would like to get their hands on Cosmos – someone whose power-hungry plans will lead George to a black hole and sure-fire deep space danger.